Cat Talk

The Secrets of Communicating with Your Cat

Sonya Fitzpatrick
THE PET PSYCHIC™

B

BERKLEY BOOKS, NEW YORK

THE BERKLEY PUBLISHING GROUP
Published by the Penguin Group
Penguin Group (USA) Inc.,
375 Hudson Street, New York, New York 10014, USA
Penguin Group (Canada), 10 Alcorn Avenue, Toronto,
Ontario M4V 3B2, Canada (a division of Pearson Penguin Canada Inc.)
Penguin Books Ltd., 80 Strand, London WC2R 0RL, England
Penguin Group Ireland, 25 St. Stephen's Green, Dublin 2, Ireland (a division of Penguin Books Ltd.)
Penguin Group (Australia), 250 Camberwell Road, Camberwell, Victoria 3124,
Australia (a division of Pearson Australia Group Pty. Ltd.)
Penguin Books India Pvt. Ltd., 11 Community Centre, Panchsheel Park,
New Delhi—110 017, India
Penguin Group (NZ), Cnr Airborne and Rosedale Roads, Albany,
Auckland 1310, New Zealand (a division of Pearson New Zealand Ltd.)
Penguin Books (South Africa) (Pty.) Ltd., 24 Sturdee Avenue,
Rosebank, Johannesburg 2196, South Africa

Penguin Books Ltd., Registered Offices: 80 Strand, London WC2R 0RL, England

PRINTING HISTORY
Berkley hardcover edition / October 2003
Berkley trade paperback edition / November 2004
Berkley trade paperback ISBN: 0-425-19816-2

The Library of Congress has catalogued the Berkley hardcover edition as follows:

Fitzpatrick, Sonya, date.
  Cat talk : the secrets of communicating with your cat / by Sonya Fitzpatrick.
    p. cm.
ISBN 0-425-19495-7
    1. Cats—Behavior—Anecdotes. 2. Cats—Psychology—Anecdotes. 3. Human-animal
communication—Anecdotes. 4. Fitzpatrick, Sonya. I. Title.

SF446.5.F48 2003
636.8—dc22   2003057780

PRINTED IN THE UNITED STATES OF AMERICA

10 9 8 7 6 5 4 3 2 1

...think that psychic readings are just for human beings, then you thought wrong. Sonya Fitzpatrick, an English-born animal lover not only psychically communicates with pets, but explains to their often frustrated owners just what's bothering them." —CBS News

Cat Talk

As all cat lovers know, there is something mysterious about the feline. The most loved cat can suddenly treat its owners to a display of haughtiness and disdain; an apparently happy cat can suddenly, for no reason, embark on an explosive chase after an invisible foe. But what is really going on in your cat's head?

Using case studies from her career as a pet psychic, Sonya Fitzpatrick gives us a unique cat's-eye view of the world. She explains what cats are thinking—and reveals what is really important to them. Sonya gives cat lovers advice on dealing with behavioral problems, gives tips on nutrition and diet, and describes how she locates missing cats. And for those who'd like to try communicating with their pet, she gives a step-by-step guide to learning cat talk. With knowledge, insight, and compassion, she teaches us to appreciate our feline companions in a wonderful new way, and most important, to speak their language . . .

Praise for Sonya Fitzpatrick

"She knows what Fido's feeling." —*Providence Journal-Bulletin*

"A combination of Dr. Dolittle and Eliza Doolittle after her transformation at the hands of Henry Higgins . . . There's no denying her charm." —*The Bradenton Herald*

"The Pet Psychic opens a new door to the world of animal interaction." —*News-Sun* (FL)

"Salem from *Sabrina, the Teenage Witch* isn't TV's only talking pet . . . Sonya Fitzpatrick chats with plenty of animals who've got dirt to dish on their owners." —*TVGuide.com*

Also by Sonya Fitzpatrick

What the Animals Tell Me

CONTENTS

Acknowledgments

I would like to express my gratitude and grateful thanks to all who have been involved from the germination of the idea for this book to the completion of the task. It is perhaps invidious to selectively single out some in particular and in doing so I offer my apologies for any sins of omission that might occur for space considerations.

To Heather McLatchie for her invaluable research contribution and technical expertise. To Nancy Yost of Lowenstein Associates for her continued interest in nurturing my literary ambitions, and for her valued suggestions and experienced insights into the intricacies of the publishing world. To Marcia Schanzmeyer for her very able assistance in so many areas, for her calming influence and for smoothing out the creative obstacle course. To my children, Sean, Patrick, and Emma, for their unfailing love and support. To my mother who taught me to believe in myself. To my dear husband, Fitz, whose somewhat stern appearance belies a heart of gold, which he opens to the entire animal world, both biped and quadruped! To my dear departed friend Diana with whom I have had the privilege and pleasure of sharing a wonderful relationship; first in this world and which now continues in the spiritual realm. To my English publisher, Gordon Wise, who commissioned this and my first book, for his support over the years, and my editor, Ingrid Connell, for all her help. To Susan Hill and Liz Davis for their work on the manuscript and Rafu Romaya for her classy design. To Naomi Fiddler for her enthusiasm, and for sharing her story of Pele. To Sarah Benny, Gina Rozner, and Elizabeth Allen for doing such a fabulous job with publicity for both books.

Introduction

THE lights begin to brighten. Television cameras trundle forward focusing on me. The realization dawns that I am no longer a guest, I am the hostess. This is *The Pet Psychic,* my own television show produced by Animal Planet.

This is not a normal television audience nor will this be a normal TV show. Half of this audience is animals—animals that are as excited as their human companions because they know there is a human present who can speak *their* language.

While waiting for the show to begin and listening to the hubbub of conversation and the cacophony of excited animal sounds, I reflect on the dramatic changes in my life since my first book, *What the Animals Tell Me,* was published in the United States, the United Kingdom, Germany, and Japan.

Since then I have been privileged to have had the opportunity of meeting with and talking to animal lovers and their pets from these and other countries throughout the world.

It is a continuing source of wonderment and inspiration to me that, despite the limitations and potential barriers of spoken language in the human world, I am able, using the universal telepathic language, to communicate with animals anywhere.

Equally satisfying has been communicating with their human companions, sometimes with difficulty, but always with humor and understanding.

In bridging the divide between human speech and animals' telepathic language, I hope and believe that I have been able to bring a new perspective and an additional dimension to many human/animal relationships.

Every country has its animal welfare problems, but there is a global commonality of love, concern, and tenderness toward animals that transcends national frontiers and social cultures.

This particular morning, I'm looking forward to meeting a studio full of animals and the humans who care for them. The audience quiets down, and I introduce myself. My name is Sonya Fitzpatrick and the stage lights blaze on.

During the next hour I talk to a buffalo, a llama, lizards, fish, dogs, rabbits, and, of course, the inevitable cat. And they all talk back. This is just a normal day for me, yet my ability to communicate with animals continues to be a source of joy.

In my work as an animal communicator I encounter a wide variety of species and derive great pleasure and satisfaction whenever I have the chance to address a problem or challenge with a new breed. However, the majority of clients who arrange a consultation with me have animal companions who are either dogs or cats.

While attempting to steer a middle course between lovers of both, I realize there are intrinsic differences between cats and dogs. I have written this particular book in an attempt to do justice to the fascinating complexities that make up the feline character.

Domesticated? Yes! Cats are, up to a point, but still lurking underneath that purring, generally pliable furry creature are marked and occasionally wild and explosive manifestations of its untamed nature.

For the dedicated feline lover, the affair with their cat can be as exciting, frustrating, and tempestuous as any human relationship. It is the observation, understanding, and inevitable compromise in the development of a trusting relationship that brings such satisfaction and long-term enjoyment for both parties.

In this book, I will deal with many examples of the problems that can develop when humans and felines interact and illustrate them from the cat's point of view.

I believe *Cat Talk* brings a new perspective for humans to consider when they encounter perplexing and sometimes apparently insoluble problems with their feline friends.

Chapter One

Early Years

I WAS born in 1940—when a new Ford car cost about five hundred dollars, the first nylon stockings went on sale in the United States, and the letter *V* (for Victory) began appearing on walls in German-occupied Belgium. My parents, Cora and Russell Smith, owned the grocery shop in an English country village, Hartwell, in Northamptonshire. My two sisters, Dawn and Coral, my brother, Gordon, and I lived among many furry and feathered friends.

I could speak to animals. I thought everyone could. It never occurred to me that I was different.

When I was eleven years old, I was diagnosed with an acute hearing problem. Perhaps that's why as a child imprisoned in my silent world, I awakened each morning "hearing and feeling" the animals' language. They were my companions and teachers. I was one of them and I understood their ways. I lived more in their world than in the human one at times, and was actually considered "backward" by some in those days before deafness and dyslexia were properly understood. It says much about my family's love and tolerance that I didn't even know I was deaf until much later in life, by which time I had become an expert lip-reader and unconsciously honed all my other senses in a way that, I'm convinced, helped me to communicate with animals. I loved their world more than mine, and I still do. I came to see my hearing "problem" as something of a gift, as it had heightened those other senses. My daughter Emma inherited the hearing trouble but by the time she was at Millfield School, things were much better understood and she was never made to feel disadvantaged.

Though my early life was shared with remarkable animals, the Midlands village where I grew up was also full of colorful humans. Some were a source of inspiration and joy to me. They made up the fabric of village life and they too adored their animals.

Grandmother Robishaw

My grandmother Emmaline Robishaw and my grandfather Frederick Smith, on my father's side, both lived close by.

I adored my grandmother. She helped me to better communicate with humans, despite my hearing loss, by teaching me to lip-read. As a young woman she had worked in the cotton mills of Lancashire where noisy machines made normal speech impossible and lip-reading had been the only way to communicate. The ability to lip-read helped me to feel connected to the human world. It's a skill I still use today.

A petite woman with high cheekbones, Grandmother Robishaw pulled her silver hair back in a chignon and always wore tailored clothes. She insisted on quality classics and complemented them by wearing a pearl necklace and earrings and a gold cameo brooch.

Grandmother shared her home with a dog named Lord Mountbatten and a superior, extremely independent feline called Gracie, named after the English singer Gracie Fields. Gracie had a pretty tabby face and liked to be tickled under her chin but could be aloof at times. She was a good judge of character and a wise animal who did not stray from Grandmother Robishaw's cottage garden.

I often stayed overnight at Grandmother's home where I had my own small bedroom with dark oak beams, white lace-trimmed curtains, and a bed with linen pillowcases trimmed with matching lace. The bed cover was hand-crocheted. The small bed was warmed with a stone bottle filled with hot water that nestled between the covers and was moved down the bed to warm my feet before I went to sleep.

Grandmother loved nature and animals. She taught me to respect and honor all creatures no matter how insignificant—ants, frogs, bees—as they all had their place in God's universe. She explained how animals, plants, and all living things work together in the fascinating pattern of nature. Grandmother nur-

tured my love of the animal kingdom and my ability to communicate there. She acknowledged my gift by making sure I had
every opportunity to observe wild creatures in their natural habi-
tats.

We spent hours together in Salcey Forest observing nature
and the animal kingdom. The forest is part of the great woodland that once stretched through the center of England and was
linked to Sherwood Forest, home of the legendary outlaw Robin
Hood. It abounded in animal life—deer, wild boar, rabbits, even
a colony of feral cats that had taken over a derelict gamekeeper's
cottage.

Gracie sometimes asked me about the wild cat Smudge who
lived in Grandmother's washhouse. Smudge was usually sad as
he had mange. Extremely wild, he'd hiss as people approached
him. Still, he liked the name Smudge, which I'd given him.
When I used it I could see a softening in his eyes.

Smudge said he felt a sense of belonging with my grandmother and me. He was quite old for a feral cat—they seldom
live as long as domestic cats. My grandmother fed him, adding
honey to his water and cod-liver oil to his food, believing they
would help his skin.

Sugar and Spice were two other feline residents of Grandmother's barn and washhouse. Spice, a male cat, was always
fighting. Then there were Pepper and Giant, both young black
cats. Their mother, Minny, watched over them. Sometimes they
would balance on our rain butt to drink from it, and stop lapping
to observe the tadpoles I'd put there.

I thought it great fun to bring back frog's spawn from the vil-

lage pond. I loved watching each tadpole grow until it was perfectly formed, swimming and separating from the jelly. At times
as many as twenty tadpoles emerged from one mass of spawn
into their new home in my grandmother's water-butt.

Grandfather and Lord Kitchener

Some days I would visit Grandfather Smith on the way home
from school. He was a handsome man, six feet tall, and had a
long moustache with the ends stiffened with wax and curled
under.

He always wore "plus fours," baggy britches rather like jodh-
purs. His socks turned over at the top where they met the plus
fours and were finished with a knitted pattern around the edge.
His jacket always matched his trousers, and was either a brown
check or a Donegal tweed. Brown leather Oxford shoes completed his ensemble.

Under his jacket he wore a starched white shirt with a stiff collar. He changed the collar each day as he had bought ten thousand detachable collars at auction and loved the idea of throwing
one away when he was finished with it. He was quite proud of
the collar purchase. He'd bought the lot at the bargain price of
five pounds, three shillings and sixpence.

Grandfather Smith was always happy to see me and often had
a list of shopping for me to do. He lived with his cat, Lord Kitchener, an independent and not overly friendly animal.

Lord Kitchener was handsome and knew it. He frequently

told me how handsome he was and that he liked his coloring—grey with large china-blue eyes. He would strut toward me and look up, waiting for me to scratch his head. He often listened in on the conversations I had with the village feral cats. He had a soft spot for wild cats since he had been feral as a kitten.

In fact, my grandfather found him in an outbuilding when he was only a few weeks old, nestled up to his dead mother, crying. Grandfather said his mother had been killed by rat poison.

"I understand your love of animals," Grandfather told me. "Lord Kitchener strikes something very deep within me and this little animal has changed my whole life. You, Sunny," he would say, "were born with these feelings toward the animal kingdom and that is a gift in itself." Apart from his horse, Lord Kitchener was the only animal my grandfather ever owned.

Grandfather was quite absentminded and Lord Kitchener was his "minder." When Grandfather misplaced anything, he would ask his trusted friend to find it. The cat would rub against his leg and walk toward the object, glancing back to make sure Grandfather was following. Often the lost item was among the clutter on top of one of three grand pianos Grandfather had in his cottage. Lord Kitchener knew which one and would jump up onto the keyboard, prancing along, pushing down the keys with his paws, playing a tune.

"What a clever chap you are to find that for me. What would I do without you?" Grandfather would say, giving the cat's head a rub. He marveled at the cat's ability to find things as well as being amused by his musical skills. The precocious creature would jump on the piano and play for pleasure when there were guests present.

My grandfather was an accomplished musician. During hot summer days the cottage door was left open and village people liked to stop and listen to Grandfather playing the piano.

There was a certain lady who stopped by more often than other people as she had her heart set on marrying Grandfather Smith. She tried to woo him with her scones, steak and kidney pies, and cakes, much to Lord Kitchener's disgust. She'd arrive at Grandfather's door, all flushed and flustered, bearing gifts.

"I made you a lovely cake, Mr. Smith," she'd say as he invited her into the cottage. Then, lowering her rather large posterior down in the rocking chair by the range, she would flash her eyes at him, but all to no avail. The lady frequently asked Grandfather Smith if he ever thought of marrying again, and insinuated that he needed a good woman "to take care of him and his home." He'd reply with raised brows and a smile, twisting his moustache with his fingers, "Who would want me?"

"You would be surprised, Mr. Smith. Maybe it's someone who's sitting in your rocking chair right now."

At that, Lord Kitchener, with an expression of annoyance, would jump up on the piano and play loudly, running over the keyboard as fast as he could, pounding on the keys.

"Can't hear myself speak. What was that you were saying, Mrs. Morgan? I can't hear you," Grandfather would murmur.

She'd soon leave, as she couldn't compete with the noise coming from the piano. When she was well outside the cottage, the cat would jump down from the piano with a look of triumph on his face. After a tickle under the chin and a conspiratorial wink, Grandfather could be heard to say, "Well done, Lord Kitchener, well done."

Lord Kitchener told me he had been with my grandfather in other lives before he came into this life in his cat body. He was psychic, as many cats are, and could see into the future. One day he told me Bessie, the old lady who lived next door, was going to die soon.

Animals learn to judge time by our routines. They know night and day by darkness and light and morning and evening by darkness turning to light or light turning to dark. I asked Lord Kitchener if Bessie would die during the night. He told me she would die during the day. He sent me a mental picture of her lying down in the yard.

Bessie was an active lady. She liked to garden even though she was in her seventies and she still used well water to drink and water her plants. Lord Kitchener told me she would die near the well. I immediately informed my grandfather and two days later he found poor old Bessie dead by the well just before lunchtime. I was sent to get Aunt Rene, the village undertaker.

On the way to her cottage, I heard several village people say how lucky Bessie was to die so quickly with her shoes on and that "the poor old spinster would go to Heaven unopened." I asked Lord Kitchener if he knew what that meant. He was as bemused as I.

Aunt Rene

Aunt Rene worked as a part-time assistant in my father's store. It was her second job that bewildered me until I got a little older and realized what the undertaker did.

Whenever she received a message at my father's shop, she would pull on her coat and run out. When that happened, we knew someone in the village had just died. Since they were already dead, I once asked her why she had to run so fast. She favored me with a stern look from her piercing brown eyes and replied, "This is a very serious business I need to tend to." Her chest puffed out as she explained that she had to get to the body while the body was still warm.

If she did not arrive soon enough, the body got cold and stiff. If the person had been, for example, sitting up in a chair when he died, Aunt Rene said the body would set like cement in the sitting position. But if she arrived within an hour of the person dying, the body was still warm and she could, with help, transfer the body onto a bed where it was easy for her to straighten out the arms and legs and ready the body for the coffin.

She added that after she washed the body, she would then stuff it. I did not realize it was just the orifices she stuffed because, when her beloved cat Tiger died, she had his whole body stuffed and put in a glass case.

I enjoyed visiting Aunt Rene and she must have liked me too, as she often invited me to tea. A spinster, she lived alone in a pretty cottage at the top of the village. The cottage had a kitchen to the rear, a sitting room at the front and an oak staircase that led up from the sitting room to her tiny bedroom where sat the glass case containing the stuffed remains of Tiger.

I enjoyed Aunt Rene's scrumptious teas. Her scones melted in my mouth, as did her delicious homemade blackberry jam. At teatime a white tablecloth with a design of cats around the edge embroidered by Aunt Rene covered the table. The matching white napkins had one big cat embroidered in the middle. The table was set with her best blue and white willow-patterned Spode china.

Aunt Rene always brought the case with Tiger's stuffed remains down from the bedroom and placed him in the middle of the table when we took tea together. She said she liked him to join us. It seemed strange to have the case there since I could still see Tiger's spirit form sitting in his old armchair. Tiger would comment to me how he had liked his physical body but that he was pleased to have left it behind since now he no longer had any pain. I would tell Aunt Rene what he was saying to me. Her kind face would soften and she would laugh and say, "Sunny, you are an inspiration and how I love your imagination."

After a saucer filled with milk, sugar, and tea had been placed by Tiger's glass case, Aunt Rene would say, "There you are, Tiger, here's your tea." Once she told me she did that because when Tiger had lived in his physical body, he had been partial to a saucer of tea each afternoon. She said he'd sit on the table waiting for her and always drink his tea with her.

As we talked, we'd include Tiger in our conversation.

"He's much prettier than any flowers you can put on the

table," Aunt Rene often commented, gazing lovingly at Tiger's glass case.

When she was doing her housework, Aunt Rene took Tiger around the house with her. If she was doing the washing up, he and his glass case would sit at the sink. If she was baking, he would sit on the table. And each night when she went to bed, she took him upstairs with her. She shared all the activities of her daily routine with Tiger, just as she had done when he was alive, so sharing afternoon tea with him was a normal occurrence. Whenever any of her friends visited her for afternoon tea, Tiger always joined in.

I once asked her why everyone in the village called her aunt Rene. "How can you be everyone's aunt?"

She stared at me for a moment as though choosing her words carefully. "To be perfectly honest and frank, my duck, everyone thinks of me that way because I lay out people's relatives when they are dead. When you have to lay out and wash a family's naked bodies, people get very close to you. So they think of me as an aunt."

After we finished tea and it was time for me to go, I'd thank Aunt Rene for inviting me and waved goodbye to Tiger. My animal retinue, consisting of my geese Daisy, Buttercup, and Primrose, and my dog, Silky, was often waiting for me in her front garden. Sometimes the geese would have eaten some of her flowers and I'd apologize to Aunt Rene. "That's okay, my duck. Hope they enjoyed them," she'd say.

As my feathery and furry friends and I made our way down the village street, the geese or Silky would sometimes comment on the unusual things humans did. For instance, stuffing animals made no sense to them. They asked if I would be stuffing them when their time came to leave.

I told them when the time came for them to visit me in their spiritual bodies, I would be able to communicate with them, just as I was doing now. I did not think it was necessary to have them stuffed. They informed me they would prefer not to be stuffed and were happy that I would be able to talk to them as I did with Tiger.

Father

Thursday and Friday were the busiest days of the week in my dad's shop. As many as ten or twelve villagers at a time crammed in, stepping around and over the sacks of potatoes and boxes of fresh vegetables and fruit that stood on the stone-slab floor.

Animals often accompanied their owners. Sometimes a dog would lift its leg and spray a sack of potatoes and then continue round the shop spraying, including over the wooden boxes where apples were stored. This infuriated Dad but since he thought the customer was always right, he would remain silent. He didn't realize the animals could pick up his telepathic rage. The angrier he got, the more they harassed him. When I tried to explain this, Dad would just roll his eyes and say, "What a vivid imagination you have." He did not realize how closely imagination and telepathy are related.

One of Dad's best customers was Canon Martin's wife. She had an amazing cat called Jeremiah who always accompanied her and her dog, Bertie, when she visited the shop. My father liked Bertie, but Jeremiah was his favorite. When Jeremiah strutted into the shop and sat by the door, my father would smile happily and cut a piece of ham into small pieces for his special "assistant."

Jeremiah quickly devoured most of the ham, leaving only a little for Bertie. After eating, he'd take up his guard position by the front door, keeping away all dogs except Bertie. If any other dog attempted entry, Jeremiah would strut forward, back arched, hissing and spitting, and smack them right across the nose. Every dog in the village felt his claws and they all backed off. He could sometimes take on as many as five dogs at a time!

Jeremiah liked working as Dad's "assistant." He was a big cat with a big ego and he liked the attention he got from the other customers. Of course, they didn't know he was doing a job of work or that Dad rewarded him with a juicy chunk of ham. Jeremiah told me he took this work quite seriously. Dad did not realize that had he not paid Jeremiah with ham, the wily feline would have gladly allowed all the village dogs into the shop to spray on whatever they liked.

Old Beat

Another of my favorite people was old Beatrice, known as Old Beat. Beat lived a mile from the village as a companion to Mrs. Weston. The two shared a thatch roofed, two hundred year-old limestone cottage that was full to the rafters with animals.

Beat's face was crisscrossed with character lines, some of

them deep with grime. One of her front teeth was missing and her skin looked weathered, but her eyes were an intense blue. Beat possessed a contagious smile and was one of the kindest, most generous people I have ever met. She would have given her last penny away if she thought someone needed it.

Though her back was bent over and she suffered from arthritis, she never complained. In winter she wore an old Harris tweed overcoat with frayed cuffs and leather patches on the elbows and wound a bright knitted woolen scarf on her head. She always wore the same old beaten-up leather boots with brown woolen stockings that wrinkled and twisted around her legs.

The cottage Beat and Mrs. Weston shared had an overgrown garden full of sunflowers, lupins, and hollyhocks. An old gate hung by a hinge; honeysuckle climbed over the dilapidated fence, and climbing pink and red roses rambled over the stone walls to frame the kitchen doorway.

Mrs. Weston spent her whole life in the living room. She was unable to climb the stairs, so she slept downstairs, sometimes hidden by the mass of animals sharing the bed with her.

Though Mrs. Weston greatly disliked children, after I'd help Old Beat push their groceries home across the fields in a rickety baby buggy, she'd consent to my being invited in for tea.

I thought their cottage a magical place. Chickens were allowed everywhere throughout the downstairs, as were Bessie and Billy, the goats who acted as gardeners and once ate several of Old Beat's jumpers. Beat kept a jackdaw, Lucky Boy, upstairs in her bedroom. Sixteen cats shared the cottage with the old ladies and they had names for all of them. Most of the cats slept

with Mrs. Weston on one of the old grey army blankets that covered her bed.

Dust lay thick throughout the house. Chickens and ducks
pecked at the cottage floor. Beat said they helped to keep it clean.
No other floor cleaning was done other than an occasion sweep
with a broom. The animals didn't seem to mind the dust and the
two old girls certainly did not.

Mother told me I should never eat or drink with Beat and
Mrs. Weston, but of course I did. I often asked mother why we
didn't live like them, with all the animals in the house. I told her
theirs was my very favorite house. It was so romantic, I thought,
to live in a cottage in a field and be so close to nature.

How wonderful, I said, that the goats and chickens helped
with the housework, and I tried to explain to Mother how she
wouldn't have to clean the house if we lived like that. She rolled
her eyes up to heaven. "When I grow up, Mother, I shall live just
like Beat and Mrs. Weston do!"

I loved being surrounded by animals inside the house and
was happy Mrs. Weston loved all animals, even though she
didn't think much of children.

Lady Alice was Mrs. Weston's favorite cat. She had raised
three litters of kittens as well as nursed and raised two wild brown
rabbits called Rosie and Snoopy. Lady Alice was a communica-
tive cat and told me she was in charge of the other animals that
roamed in and out of the house including chickens, dogs, rabbits,
goats, and Lucky Boy. They all respected her authority.

One night Mrs. Weston fell out of bed and broke her arm.
Lady Alice, who always slept on Mrs. Weston's pillow, ran up-

stairs to alert Old Beat. Beat shared her room with her dog, Nelly Dean, and the jackdaw. Lady Alice couldn't open the door or even wake Nelly Dean, the dog.

In desperation, Lady Alice managed to climb on top of the marble washstand outside Old Beat's door and push the basin and jug on to the floor, smashing them. When Beat opened her bedroom door there was Lady Alice meowing and running down the stairs. Beat hurried down to find Mrs. Weston lying on the floor, shivering from the cold and shock and in great pain.

Spud, another village feline who lived with the Webster family, was another cat who showed his ingenuity and intelligence by alerting his family to danger. In those days, fireplaces were the only form of heating. At night people would damp down the fire but keep it smoldering. During the night, a hot coal fell out of the Webster's fire onto the hearth rug. Spud alerted Mr. and Mrs. Webster by running upstairs, jumping on the bed, and standing over their heads meowing. When they woke up, wondering what the hell was happening, he ran downstairs and jumped onto the piano, scampering over the keys, creating a terrible racket.

Mr. and Mrs. Webster hurried downstairs to see what the commotion was all about, to find smoke filling the sitting room. The rug was scorching and would have soon caught fire if Spud had not alerted them. Within weeks, the village had two feline heroes.

$\mathcal{M}$y Gift

As I grew older, I began to realize not all people loved animals the way my grandmother, Old Beat, and I did, nor did many people have much idea how intelligent animals were. I also saw that my ability to communicate with animals was difficult for people to believe. People said I was imagining things. They couldn't understand what I meant when I said animals spoke, but spoke in a different way from humans by using pictures, sense, and emotions.

Even my family found it hard to believe I could "hear" with all my senses and emotions and receive animal messages with my physical body. Even as a child, I knew how intense cat sense and feelings are compared to human ones. I could see through their eyes and think as they did. I even shared their sense of humor and laughed with them. As I grew older I began to understand such experiences were beyond most human's capabilities and realize that my hearing "problem" probably helped me to communicate with animals.

My life of gossiping and laughing with animals, both wild and domestic, continued until one dark day in December. I was at my grandmother's house on a Sunday morning just before Christmas when I woke early with a strange, unsettling feeling. While getting dressed and tiptoeing downstairs, I tried not to notice the unease which kept jabbing at me. In the past when this dread came over me, something bad always happened.

After pouring the feral cats some milk, the feeling became

stronger. I began to panic—to question myself. Perhaps I'd forgotten to lock up the outbuilding where the geese stayed. I dreaded something happening to my geese. The panic grew worse, and I started to run. As the shed came into view, I relaxed because I could see the doors were closed and my friends were safe.

Sunday was my day to visit my friend Hilda at Folly Farm. We'd saddle up the horses and enjoy a two-hour ride. I pushed my anxiety aside. After my ride, I had to hurry home for lunch. In those days, Sunday lunch was an occasion.

I wasn't hungry because of the fear I'd felt all morning, but I supposed Mother was preparing our usual Sunday lunch of roast beef with Yorkshire pudding and fresh vegetables, followed by homemade apple pie and custard. Lunch this particular Sunday proved to be one of the saddest in my life as Mother placed a platter of roast goose on the table. I was overcome and ran sobbing from the table, searching frantically for the rest of my geese. I found them hanging upside-down from a rafter in the barn.

My small goose family was no longer with me on this physical plane. I knew then why I had been uneasy and fretful all day and why I'd been unable to communicate with any of my friends.

Raising food was a way of life for my father. He did not consider my geese as friends. He had no sentiment there—to him they were not even pets. They were farm animals, to be used for food, and in this case, as Christmas presents. Since it was just after the war, rationing was still in force and meat was in short supply. What my father did was routine for him, logical.

Inside, I knew Primrose, Daisy, and Buttercup were happy and no longer felt any pain. But the shock and grief of their deaths was so great, I closed off the ability to communicate with animals or spirits. I never wanted to risk that much pain ever again. It would be years before I was able to communicate with animals in that special way again.

The Middle Years

My childhood was for the most part happy, almost idyllic, but I knew that one day I would leave village life behind to find out what the wider world had in store for me. My very limited exposure to the fashion business came in Northhampton where I worked part-time in a dress shop. It was interesting and enjoyable work and the proprietor was complimentary about my modeling efforts. He said that he thought I could have a career in fashion if I wanted, and instinctively, I knew this would be the catalyst for dramatic changes in my life.

I was accepted as a trainee by a respected national modeling agency. At seventeen, I said farewell to village life and left to begin my training in London. In my state of excitement and enthusiasm I thought I would be an overnight sensation but I was brought down to earth very quickly by my initial exposure to the rigors and discipline imposed at the agency and the severity of the curriculum.

In those days, the training and discipline necessary to become a model was exacting and arduous, contrasting markedly with the instant rise to fame that has launched many supermodels in today's fashion world. Great attention was paid to social etiquette, deportment, grace, and personal grooming, even during the training course. There was definitely no turning up wearing jeans or casual clothes. At the time, the recognized word to describe a fully trained graduate of a fashion model agency was *mannequin*, and a mannequin was expected to project and embody all these qualities both on the runway and in her personal lifestyle. It was a respected and admired vocation.

While I expected that good fortune and financial success were just around the corner, I had to face up to the immediate problem of survival in a large city by finding ways to earn money, so I embarked on a variety of part-time evening or weekend jobs. My adventures and limited success in these areas could not be considered a good omen for the future.

My job as a cinema usherette lasted for only one evening when I succeeded in seating the majority of the customers in the wrong seats and because I used my flashlight to highlight embarrassed couples that were not exactly engrossed in watching the movie. I also interviewed for a "social secretary" position in a famous West End nightclub, but declined when I found out that the job entailed greeting guests wearing a smile and practically nothing else.

I did enjoy one part-time job working evenings in a coffeehouse in the theatre district in the West End of London. Apart from tourists and theater-goers, many actors and actresses came in late in the evening and were very friendly. But soon I was working full-time as a fashion model. I traveled to capitals of major European countries and to the United States. I went to film premieres, where I met famous actors and actresses.

Felines were also a part of my fashion career. I used to model for a small, exclusive boutique in Beauchamp Place in Knightsbridge. The young man who owned the shop was called Charles and he and his partner, Leslie, were the proud companions of two very beautiful Siamese cats named Beethoven and Mozart, who almost seemed to be business partners. Leslie designed many of the dresses himself, and I loved his use of silk in beautiful bright colors. Over the years we became good friends.

The store had an exclusive clientele and Leslie and Charles said clients' cats were always welcome. During the week of the fashion shows, champagne flowed and pearls were worn with every garment that went down the runway. "Girls, girls, don't forget your pearls," Leslie would say. He always had a long cigarette holder and he came into our fitting rooms where we were changing with rows of pearls around his neck. If we'd forgotten our pearls, he would take one off and place it in our hands, saying, "Darlings, you could all go out on the runway naked but you would still look elegant if you just wore your pearls."

Mozart and Beethoven were their babies and they always wore pearl or diamond collars with bow ties on the front. They were the mascots of the store and we loved them. They would walk on the runways with us, getting more attention than the models and stealing the show. The models were all cat lovers as well. Before you were allowed the privilege of modeling for their store, Charles and Leslie's first question was, "Do you love cats?" They would introduce you to the cats and ask their opinion. This could be nerve-wracking for some of the models, as the cats might gaze with quiet disdain and stalk away. But if you were eating smoked salmon sandwiches, you were their best friend.

The cats responded to the intelligent cooperation of their human companions and knew their responsibility as part of the store. They were participants in the shop's success and many people would come in just to see them. A restaurant owner across the road would often send prawns or cooked fish over for them.

One time, Leslie was showing dresses and there were big claw marks where one of the cats had climbed the dress but he was fine about it. Whatever their cats did was perfect. He thought it just added to the appeal of the dress. "Doesn't it look beautiful?" he would say.

I could have continued in the modeling world for many years but romance intervened. I married at twenty and had three wonderful children, Sean, Patrick, and Emma, in rapid succession. Living then in Buckinghamshire, it was easy to visit my parents in the village just across the county border. But the marriage failed, and I returned to London with the children and resumed my modeling career.

Combining the role of fashion model and mother was an exacting and exhausting business but I was still able to enjoy many of the social aspects of London life. I was heartened by the fact that I was now in demand as a more mature model and I had no trouble finding work. I also was able to resume friendships with some of the models I had known earlier in my career and the old spirit of camaraderie was still there. We combined professionalism with good humor and lots of fun.

Occasionally, during the interludes between fashion shows I honed my knitting and design skills and began producing knitted jackets of my own unusual design. When I was modeling at Harrods I was approached by the chief buyer about where I had bought my jacket, and when I told her it was my own work she suggested I go into business. I was pleasantly surprised to find I was able to get my designs in many of the stores I had modeled in. All the designs were in my head and I translated them to patterns that were given to outworkers who initially produced curious results until we were able to get our styles in sync.

During 1976 I met Denis Fitzpatrick, "Fitz", the individualistic Ulsterman who was to become my second husband. Our relationship blossomed during the summer of the Queen's Silver Jubilee, when the whole country seemed to be caught up in the mood of celebration and goodwill. We set up home in Baker Street, happy to enjoy all the cultural advantages of living in central London along with the almost villagelike atmosphere of the Marylebone area and the wide spaces of Regent's Park. It was a very happy time, and I enjoyed combining family life with part-time modeling work. Over the past twenty-five years I have sometimes recalled the humorous words of Fitz's delightful mother who'd said God help the woman who got him! But despite a somewhat tempestuous relationship we have endured, secure in the knowledge that each of us has brought to the other an acceptable level of order and discipline—well, almost!

We had a house in Vence in the south of France, where we spent several holidays a year. When we visited I would often shop in Nice or Cannes and there too I was approached about my jackets. Before long I was able to supply many of my designs to exclusive shops in both cities as well as to a shop in Monte Carlo in Monaco.

An aspect of my old affinity with cats followed me on these travels. Our house was in the older part of the town and overlooked the Mediterranean. It was small and quiet, with flagstones on the floor and I just loved it. I used to feed all the neighborhood cats as many people there left cats to fend for themselves. My neighbors always said they knew when I was coming because the cats would be sitting outside the door waiting for me the day before I arrived.

When I went into town to shop or to the café, I would leave the house open and on one occasion, I returned home to discover a headless rat that had been left in the hallway as a thank-you from one of my feline charges. I always worried about those cats when I returned home to England.

A few years later after a series of operations and another move, I decided to wind up my design business. My journey to living in America began when my husband, Fitz, and I met an American couple who moved into our Baker Street apartment block one Christmas. We became very good friends. After they returned to Connecticut, I visited them when modeling assignments took me to New York.

They came back and forth to London regularly and our friendship endured. When they later decided to move from Connecticut to Houston, Texas, I visited and loved it. I had a feeling then that I would live in America, even though it was almost eight years before I actually did so. The warm weather was a draw as much as anything and things happened there that I still find myself marveling about today—only in America.

Not long after our friends moved, there was a recession in England and we were hit hard. Fitz's business suffered and I became quite ill; residual complications from my pregnancies led to a series of operations culminating in an early hysterectomy. It was time to take stock and prepare a recovery program. We decided that Emma and I would move to Texas where I planned to open an etiquette studio while Fitz would try to sort the business out in England and join us later. I'd come to believe that a real opportunity lay in Houston. For Americans the idea of continuing education and self-help is a way of life, and I reckoned I could make a success of a studio that offered a range of courses in the field of enhancing business and social self-confidence. Most friends in England tried to dissuade us but I told Emma to pay no attention, that we could do it, and we did.

After several successful years in business in Houston, I was drawn back to communicating with animals as my soul's work, and writing the first book about it set everything in motion for that to be my new focus. I had a client in New York who called me because of problems with her dog that seemed insoluble despite expert advice. After I spoke to him, he returned to normal and she was astonished.

Afterward, she called and offered to arrange consultations if I would go to New York. She invited me to Fire Island, where she had a vacation home. We had to take a ferry from Manhattan and everyone on the boat with us had their animals with them.

Only when we reached the island did I realize they were all coming to see me. She had booked me out for three days.

A top literary agent was on board and asked about me. She subsequently called and said she wanted me to write a book. I wrote a proposal and visited seven New York publishers at each of which I spoke to the pets of several members of staff. This created tremendous interest and the book was duly published not only in the United States but also in the United Kingdom, Germany, and Japan.

Since then my life has changed dramatically and is now entirely devoted to furthering the better understanding and development of the human/animal relationship in all its forms, but with particular emphasis on improving animal welfare.

Chapter Two

The World Through
a Cat's Eyes

MANY people ask me how I speak to a cat. They want to know what the cat understands of the human world and how his mind works.

My ability to speak to felines is one we can all cultivate. What I do is not magic although many of my clients see it that way. The most valuable tools needed are imagination, trust, and the understanding that we are much more than just human forms.

Looking back to my childhood, I realize I lived in a world of imagination and took for granted my ability to speak to the village animals. To me it seemed quite normal to engage in conversation with delightful animal companions. Although later in life I came to appreciate what I was doing as a child was transcending the normal barriers of communication between different species, at the time I simply accepted my ability.

I spent endless hours in this pursuit and, although I occasionally spoke verbally to the animals, most exchanges were through pictures in a telepathic link. I spoke to the animals with my thoughts, which they picked up and transmitted back to me, along with pictures, feelings, emotions, and other signals I was able to receive through my physical body.

I knew their likes and dislikes, how they felt about humans and each other, and I came to appreciate the close similarities between animals and humans in the way we display emotions and feelings. Joy, elation, happiness, sadness, anger, jealousy, and practically every other emotional trait was just as apparent in my animal companions as in the human inhabitants of the village.

Naturally, as with humans, there were subtle differences in how individual species and animals projected these characteristics. None intrigued me more than the felines in the villages. To this day, the study of the unique qualities cats possess is a source of keen interest and enjoyment. Therefore, in order to understand the cats' "language," we must begin to get in touch with our intuitive self and be guided by our instincts.

Because it is normal for humans to speak verbally, we underestimate the visualization process that is behind spoken language. The feline uses a rich mixture of pictures, senses, and feelings. If we are to learn their language we should not only attempt to appreciate and employ the same tools of their process of communication, but we must also be guided by our own instincts, intuitions, and emotions.

To begin the journey into your cat's world, you will not be using verbal language. You will be using the same techniques you use when speaking, but you will hear the words in your head. In the silence that ensues, listen, sense, imagine, and feel what's happening around you.

Clear your mind of all other distractions and you will gradually become aware of an inner stillness. Let this develop naturally. Do not attempt to hurry the process. The more tranquil and relaxed your body and mind are, the more successful you will be in tuning in to your feline's thoughts.

Rediscover the unbridled imagination you possessed during childhood, but which, with time and involvement in the adult world, has probably lost its vividness and originality.

Let us start with the premise that the feline uses all his body and mental facilities in "talking" and that we can use our imagination to project our communicating with him by adopting a simulated feline form. To communicate fully, we must imagine we're in the cat's physical form.

This requires you to use your imagination to experience sight, smell, and hearing as your feline does. In doing so, you will harness the power of your mind's energy as well as that of your imagination. You will use your newly acquired physical form to speak and receive the feline's telepathic language. Now, step into your cat body and feel the world as your feline does.

Imagining

Start by kneeling on the floor, hands also resting there. Your legs and feet become your back legs and paws, your arms and hands your front legs and paws. From this position the world assumes a totally different perspective from the one you have been used to.

Bring your nose in close contact with the floor and begin to experience strong, sometimes strange smells. Imagine you are using your nose to identify and recognize your human's scent as well as the distinctive odor of other felines. You are now in the process of identifying cats and humans by scent rather than by sight, as felines do.

In your new role as a cat, your sight has also changed. You have a wide range of vision and the ability to gauge distances with much greater accuracy. Seeing in the dark is easy and you have gained the hunting and stalking prowess of the feline.

Along with these changes, you will also be aware of other differences in your cat body. A network of nerves runs throughout your physical cat form. Called sensory receptors, these nerve endings embedded in the surface of your skin are ultrasensitive and give you information about anything that touches your skin. These enable you to feel even the vibrations from noise on your physical form without being in direct contact with the noise source.

Weather changes are no mystery to you. You become aware of weather disturbances in advance through changes in the atmospheric pressure and through the earth's magnetic fields. You feel static buildup long before a storm arrives.

Imagine you have whiskers. Your whiskers are sensitive enough to pick up air movements. You use them to judge the width of an opening before venturing through.

Slowly put your awareness on your forelegs. Feel that you have sensory receptors running through your legs to assist in jumping and judging landings skillfully. These sensory receptors are also vital to you when stalking prey.

Imagine how it feels to have a tail. As you now bring your awareness to your new tail, understand it will help you to balance when climbing and jumping.

In this imaginative, spiritual world, as you "become" a cat, the changes you are imagining will change your life. You are learning what it feels like to be a cat, and you are enabling yourself to enter and share his world.

As you embrace these physical changes, you will begin to know how sensitive your cat body is and your awareness of the feline's silent language will sharpen. You will start to understand there is another way of speaking, using all your faculties rather than just your verbal skills. By using your imagination, you are preparing to communicate mentally, physically, and spiritually with your feline.

As you enter the world of the cat you will come to admire, still more, the complex and fascinating makeup of the domestic feline. You will learn how, with infinite cleverness, they combine the wonderful attributes that make them delightful companions, while still preserving and maintaining their mystery and dignity.

Take as much time as an aspiring Hollywood actor would take to practice these exercises. With patience and diligence, you will have no sense of absurdity or artifice when doing this exercise. That is an important step forward in your quest to achieve real, new communication skills.

Energy

Energy in its purest form is the life force of the universe that flows around us and through us. Your body and your cat's body is energy arranged in solid form.

All living things—humans, animals, plants, trees—emit energy. Our mind is our "radio" control tower, receiving and transmitting electromagnetic energy.

Animals communicate telepathically using their mind energy to transmit pictures, thoughts, and feelings. Humans do this also although most of us are unaware of it. This stream of mind energy that we put out through the electromagnetic fields of the earth's plane is what animals tap in to for communication.

We are all accustomed to picking up the telephone and speaking to family and friends over long distances. Cats do the same thing, but instead of using the telephone, they are using the natural elements of the magnetic fields that run through the universe.

A mind energy link is not broken even though the physical bodies may be some distance apart. This is how it is possible for you to speak to your animal from a distance. There is no separation by time or space when you speak telepathically.

When I talk to a client in Japan from the United States, I use the telephone and my voice to my client and I can speak verbally. When I speak to the feline, I use mental pictures in addition to all my sensory and intuitive faculties. The cat is attuned to the magnetic energy lines throughout the universe. In effect, he is waiting on the end of his "telephone" line to talk to me by picking up the energy my physical form is transmitting like a radio wave.

I tune in to the feline with both mind energy and body energy. I send the message that I am listening telepathically and then I start to receive his language, using my imaginary cat physical form and all of my faculties. I receive pictures, feelings, emotions, and thoughts and I am able to interpret what he's telling me. I acknowledge what he has said and send a reply.

Many scientists wonder how animals know when their owner is coming home. Perhaps you've had a dog or cat sit by the door around the time you were coming home. It's really quite simple.

Humans and animals are transmitting energy out like a radio tower. Animals can tune in to our vibrations. The cat receives the pictures and feelings of happiness you broadcast as you anticipate coming home. When you're in the car, the cat feels your frustration at traffic jams. When you travel, you are transmitting pictures of your surroundings and the feelings they invoke. Your cat tunes in to these and knows exactly when you will arrive home.

You can speak to your cat if he's curled up on your lap at home by the fire, if you're at your office, or even if you take a holiday in Australia. No matter where you are, you can still speak to your feline. If you are going to be late and arriving in darkness, then tell him by thinking of darkness. That thought and picture will be transmitted to your feline. Remember, he knows time by your routine and by the sequence of darkness for night and light for day.

One of the most important things I tell people at my seminars is, while attempting to establish telepathic communication with their cat, they must not dismiss any feeling, thought, or image that comes to them. Always acknowledge everything you receive. Welcome the images and ideas that flow telepathically. They often contain valuable information that can give you insight into your pet's thinking.

Everything needed for telepathic communication is within the mind and emotions of humans. But most of the time we are so busy working and so preoccupied with the cares of everyday living that we don't take the time to get in touch with our inner senses. Those feelings, ideas, thoughts, and pictures that come to us unbidden when we are relaxed and quiet are often our feline's way of communicating with us.

If you have sent out a thought to your cat and you suddenly receive a picture or hear a word spoken inside your mind, you have succeeded in getting through and are now receiving a response. Trust your imagination and do not dismiss images and feelings. As you practice and become more adept, you will receive all sorts of signals and pictures.

When you attempt telepathic communication with your feline, it is very important that your body, mind, and feelings work together. As you think, a picture forms. The picture must match the thought. Do not send out one message with your mind and another with your emotions. Match the feeling with the picture of what you want the cat to do, otherwise it will confuse your cat and defeat your attempt to communicate.

For example, if your cat is fighting with another cat in your home or a cat that has trespassed on your cat's territory and you want this to stop, picture him stopping the fight as you verbally ask him to do so.

Also think what could be causing the fighting. If it is in the home, perhaps it is something you have done without realizing it, such as making a fuss over one cat and not over another, or changing one cat's food by putting it on a diet. Cats are very much like children and will act up if they feel neglected.

Send your picture messages with your thoughts. Imagine you're in the physical form of the cat so he can understand you, because he uses his entire physical form to receive your message.

Send out the picture of him fighting then quickly follow that with a feeling of kindness and envision your cat just observing the other cat. Imagine you are in his cat body seeing through his eyes, looking and feeling calm as you observe the other feline. Feel all four of your paws on the ground. Feel that you want to attack but don't move your paws. Then feel your cat body retreat and walk away.

Project calmness at all times. He will receive the feeling of calmness and love, and the message from your body, as you transmit it from your physical form to his.

*D*on't Worry About Success

Several factors can affect the success of your newly learned form of communication. If you are not relaxed and focused, your telepathic communication may not be clear. Also, your cat may have difficulty in communicating telepathically if he is preoccupied with something else like chasing a mouse or eating. If you don't make yourself clear, he will not pay any attention to you.

You can hone your telepathic skills every day by talking to your feline wherever he is. You have a direct link on his "telephone line" and he can hear your silent language, so speak to him often. If you go on a business trip or holiday, he will still be able to hear you. Always feel the emotion of love as you send your message. Talking to him as you go about your routine will enhance your ability.

It is my belief that humans are all born with telepathic communication and, if we did not have the faculty of speech, we would all be speaking telepathically just as felines and all the rest of the animal kingdom do.

*R*elaxation and Visualization Techniques to Help You Communicate with Your Feline

First, find a quiet place and make sure the telephone is turned off. Spend about five minutes preparing yourself to communicate with your cat. Sit down and close your eyes. Breathe deeply.

Feel the whole of your body relaxing. Deep breathing will help you feel peaceful. If you have problems relaxing after a few minutes, don't worry. Just go straight into the exercise.

Start to think outward, toward your cat. Do not force yourself. If your cat is sleeping, he is totally relaxed. This is a good state for you to be able to reach his subconscious.

Some people like to focus on a particular object to help clear their mind. You can sit in the yoga position with legs crossed or sit in a comfortable chair or lie on the bed. Concentrate on your breathing. Take several deep breaths, using your diaphragm, not just the top part of your lungs.

Think of your pet. Imagine his appearance. Imagine you are a feline. Relax your arms and hands as you continue to breathe deeply, then relax your neck and shoulders. Be aware of the wonderful feeling traveling throughout your new cat body as you breathe.

Visualize a cat's physical form. Your arms are now your front legs and your legs have become back legs. Your hands become your front paws, your feet your back paws. Sense the claws within your paws.

Imagine your new cat body is highly sensitive. Feel your ears tuned to a heightened hearing and be aware of using your nose to identify smells. Use your mind to speak to and connect with your internal organs. Put your thoughts on your heart, kidneys, liver, intestines, lungs, bladder, blood, bones, and tissues. Connect with each organ. Be aware of the energy from each of these organs, as each of them has consciousness. Be disciplined and set aside some time each day to practice. If possible start with the relaxation exercise and move on to the eight visualization procedures that follow.

Follow these simple steps:

1. Picture your feline. If you have more than one cat, just think of the one you want to speak to. As you think of the cat, the thought and picture go out telepathically and the cat receives the image from you.

2. Visualize your cat as you say his name.

3. Feel the emotion of love as you think of your cat. He will receive the feeling from you.

4. Ask your feline if there is anything he would like to tell you. Imagine your feline sending you back a reply.

5. Ask your feline if there is anything you can do for him. Always acknowledge any image or thought that may come into your mind in the way of an answer and feel the emotion of love as you do this. Acknowledge whatever you receive.

6. Continue to ask questions. Don't keep repeating the same one. For example, if you ask if he would like a new dish, then ask how he likes his food.

7. Continue to ask questions and trust your imagination.

8. When you think you have received an answer back, acknowledge the answer. It may be a thought that

comes into your mind or a picture or a slight twinge of pain.

Do have your cat in the room with you while you are practicing your communication skills. This way you can sometimes see a physical response from your cat, particularly if you visualize your cat's favorite food. Imagine how the food smells and concentrate on sending the delicious tastes and a feeling of happiness to your cat. You may find, as some of my clients do while performing this exercise, that the cat bounds across the room to his food dish or jumps onto your lap meowing.

Remember, the first time your feline companion hears your telepathic communication, it could be quite a surprise and he may get very excited.

Whatever you feel, sense, hear, or experience during your communication, trust it. Don't question, just trust your imagination and your intuitive sense and feelings as he whispers his silent language to you.

As you continue practicing these exercises, you will become more skilled in telepathic communication. You can communicate with as many animals as you wish. They will all hear the vibrations. Just keep talking, hearing the words in your head. No effort is required. Thoughts travel fast.

Be disciplined and set aside some time each day to practice. Try this exercise for two weeks and then go on to the next one. Be disciplined and optimistic; allow time to follow the relaxation and visualization procedures outlined above. After a time you will be able to talk to your cat at any time and from any distance.

Trusting Your Physical Senses

Don't be disappointed if you do not achieve success the first few times you try these exercises. Some cats take a while to get used to hearing you. But if you continue to practice, you will eventually succeed.

ℋow to Talk Your Cat Into Staying Within His Yard

If, for instance, you no longer want your cat to go out of your yard, you must use your physical body as well as thoughts to help convey the message. Imagine you are a cat walking around the yard. See how the yard looks through your cat's eyes. Then tell him with your thoughts to stay inside the yard and then feel and picture your cat body staying there.

Feel that your body is no longer going to jump over the fence. See yourself and feel your paws wanting to jump but staying on the ground. Your cat will receive a message from your legs and paws saying you don't want him to go outside your yard. Visualize inside the yard only.

Your thoughts are transmitting out to him. You must tell him why you don't want him to leave the yard. Think of the danger and say the words in your head. He will receive the message.

To explain the dangers he can encounter outside your yard, feel and imagine yourself inside his cat body. Imagine that you are the cat being chased by two big dogs. Feel with your cat body what this would be like. Hear a dog growl and feel the dog hold-ing you down. Feel pain as teeth bite into your cat body.

Feeling this terrible pain is crucial to the exercise because this is a way of warning the feline of the dangerous, horrendous risks. As you think, you will automatically form pictures. It is impor-tant to use your imagination and physical cat form along with the emotion of fear as you feel the pain.

Tell him with your thoughts why you worry about him leaving the yard. Then feel yourself staying inside the yard. Tell him this could happen to him if he does not listen to you. Always be pos-itive with your messages and thoughts. In fact, you may receive a subtle message back from your feline, one of alarm or fear. If so you will know your cat is transmitting back a message of ac-knowledgment. Tell him with your thoughts that you have heard him, and that smart cats stay in the garden.

Send the message more than once, then tell him how much you love him and send him love. If you focus too much on his leaving the yard, you will actually be putting out pictures of him doing this, so be aware that now you must visualize him staying inside the yard.

Remember to put out positive pictures (and feelings to match) of what you want from him; otherwise, he will do the op-posite. If you put out all the right pictures and emotions, and use your physical cat body to tell him to stay in the yard, you will find your cat will not leave your yard again.

When you feel your message has been received, stay motion-less with your paws on the ground. Feel yourself stretching and walking back into the house. Feel the sun warming your cat body. Feel all the emotions of happiness and contentment you expect your cat to feel. By being aware of this happiness in your cat form as you lie inside the yard, safe and secure, you are transmitting all the right signals for him to understand.

Finally, communicate to him that he's clever!

You will find, once your physical body responds, that you will start to experience what your cat is feeling. When you feel pain or inexplicable discomfort, don't dismiss it. Learn to listen to your cat body. If you have pain in your right leg, this would relate to your cat's right hind leg. Pain in your left hand would relate to your cat's left paw.

This ability to communicate physical feelings telepathically will help you to know what is wrong with your pet before the vet does.

Now you are speaking with your mind energy. You are speaking with your emotional and physical body and your intuitive senses, just as the animals do. Their language is subtle and silent. If you hope to master telepathic communication, learn to trust your feelings, senses, and imagination. Be open to all the signals your animal friends are transmitting to you.

Trust your imagination. With practice and concentration, many of you will be able to tune in to the telepathic communication channel your cats use.

If you do not experience telepathic communication with your cat, you can still achieve much when spoken communication is delivered with love, gentleness, and positive energy. In this way, your cat will always be assured of your love, which will go a long way to eliminating common behavioral problems before they start.

Animals Enrich Our Lives

Sharing our home with thirteen animals is a revelation. Being able to communicate nonverbally with my own animals, and hearing them communicate with each other and with me is a constant joy and enriches my life.

Not a day passes that I don't thank God for my gift. I love all my animals and the sharing of my feelings and experiences with my animal friends. I have become very sensitive to their thoughts and feelings and know, at times, how similar to humans' feelings their feelings can be.

I have within my family five cats including Abby, Rosie, and her three kittens, Dante, Polly, and Molly. When we rescued Rosie from living the life of a feral cat, she was unable to feed herself, she was pregnant, undernourished, and living in fear. I could feel her fear as she remembered the hunger and the exhaustion from lack of food and water. Rosie knew she was now safe; no harm could come to her kittens, now she was communicating with me. She constantly thanked me for helping her and giving her a home. I told her it was a joy to have her with us. She told me that she had not encountered a human who could communicate with her before.

After a while, she began to tell me her fears for her kittens, had they been born at the trailer park where we found her. Sometimes male cats that did not belong to the group of cats at the park visited the trailer park. They could kill her kittens if she was to leave her young alone while she hunted for food.

She told me about a cat that had kittens underneath a timber shed and how the kittens smelled. It was not like a cat smell. The kittens were riddled with fleas. They next day they lay still and stiff and still the fleas were running over them. Their mother had been unable to save them.

Rosie finished telling me the story. She was upset about the kittens, but cats accept death, because they know that when they leave their physical plane, they survive in the spirit world. I stroked Rosie, reassuring her once again that her kittens would be safe and that could not happen to her now that she had us to take care of them all.

Rosie's pregnancy was trouble-free. She spent the last part in the guest room and my comfortable office, on a down-filled quilt in a dark cupboard. She informed me that it was her nest and her quilt was filled with the scent of her body.

She gave birth on the sofa with towels underneath her. After giving birth to Dante, she picked him up, not by using the neck, but by his middle and moved him to the safety of the cupboard. Then she came back to the sofa until the birth of the second kitten, Polly. This time she picked up Polly by the proper neck hold before moving her. Two hours later Molly was born and Rosie moved her into the nest.

As a very young, inexperienced first-time mother, it was not until she had given birth to her third kitten, Molly, that she began enjoying and suckling them. From then on, the only time she moved from them was to use the litter box. The devotion and love Rosie had for her kittens continued. Rosie played gently with them and they loved to play with her tail and each other.

Rosie even continued to let the kittens attempt to suckle after they had been weaned to solid food.

At times, she would push them away when their claws were sharp and their sharp teeth inflicted pain. It was only after she was spayed that the suckling ceased—Rosie became reluctant to allow them to suckle and discouraged them firmly.

We decided that we would keep Dante, but that if a good home could be found, Polly and Molly would go there together, as they were inseparable. Rosie informed me she was happy for them to leave until the day approached. I told Rosie we had found a human family for Polly and Molly and she would be meeting them very soon. Over the next few days, Rosie became very depressed and sad. She told me that the thought of her kittens leaving was making her unhappy, that she loved them and wanted them to stay.

I explained to Rosie that both Fitz and I now felt the same way, that we could not bear the thought of being without them and this was not going to happen. She transmitted back happiness and relief.

She then went on to tell me, and again, I could feel the sadness, "I lost my mother and miss her but she is dead." I was unprepared for the emotion Rosie transmitted to me. She was feeling the same way at the thought of losing her babies as she had when her mother died. Again I reassured her that her two girls would be staying with us and we were all a family together.

The next day Rosie was her happy and affectionate self. Nothing was going to change for her and her young. Dante, Polly, and Molly were playing rough and tumble, following each other's tails and Rosie was joining in the fun from time to time.

A few days later, she was with me in the bedroom. My bedroom is on the ground floor and I opened the French doors and walked out onto the terrace to sit in the early-morning Texas sunshine to drink my coffee and write. Rosie joined me and disappeared into the garden. I was engrossed in my writing until I decided to take the dogs out for a walk.

When I arrived back from walking the dogs, I entered my bedroom on my way to take a shower. I heard a meow and went to see what was happening. Lying on my white tiled bathroom floor were three dead lizards. Rosie was sitting by the door, thanking me once again for allowing her kittens to remain as part of our family. I told her I appreciated her kind thoughts but she did not have to bring me gifts, as lizards were much nicer when they were living.

The next trauma in Rosie's life came a few weeks later. My daughter, Emma, came to visit. Emma always sleeps in the guest suite adjacent to my office. Rosie and her kittens live upstairs and enjoy running along a gallery that connects to other rooms. For the first few months Rosie and the kittens were content to spend most of their time on the top floor of the house, where, as my home is very open, California style, they could see the ground floor area through the railings on the gallery.

Every evening after dinner Fitz and I invariably relax over coffee in the lounge and enjoy an hour of quality time with our family of animals. I have used the word *relax* but to an observer the spectacle of seven dogs and one cat in a fun mood, with no restrictions on how they choose to enjoy themselves, a better description might be *excited and uncontrolled chaos.*

When Rosie became a member of our extended family she did not participate in these frenzied shenanigans and as she progressed further into her pregnancy she was quite happy with her own company as she waited for the births. For several months after that she was also fully occupied with administering to her kittens' every need and instilling the discipline and behavioral traits that feline mothers teach so well. We also made a point of spending considerable time with Rosie and her family to begin the process of integrating them into our larger family. This was a fascinating time to watch their distinctive personalities and characters develop and the interaction between the kittens and their mother.

From the very beginning, Dante had the most adventurous nature. He was bold and confident and very affectionate, always on hand to help his more timid sisters. Then, as the kittens developed their physical skills and curiosity, we began to notice each evening that we had an audience watching us from the gallery area and we became excited, wondering how they would begin the final integration process.

Rosie continued to view the proceedings from the stairs and could not be coaxed to join in. I was concerned at this growing isolation and I also became aware of a change in her attitude toward the kittens, who had been spayed and neutered by then. When I saw Rosie hissing and spitting at Dante I felt this was going well beyond the normal pattern of development where the maternal instincts are eventually submerged to encourage independence in maturing offspring.

I had to connect to Rosie to find out why she felt this way. I explained that I wanted to know why she was so upset with them. She quickly told me that her kittens left her alone and no longer wanted to spend time in her company. She was very upset and confused as to why they did not need her now. She had been a good mother and she now felt abandoned by her young cats. This explained the transformation in her behavior toward them.

I realized Rosie was feeling the same as a human mother often does when her children grow up and become independent and she feels that she is not wanted in some way. I explained this to Rosie and told her that when my own children grew up they had become interested in other activities. Similarly, it was okay for her own babies to become independent of her as they matured.

I also added that I, too, missed my children being close to me but they were grown up and liked to do things for themselves. We all had to adjust and accept the changes, I said. She still felt deprived of their attention so I stressed that we all lived together here and asked her to try and enjoy her time now that she was not so busy taking care of them. They would still need her in a different way.

That night Rosie came to my bedroom and I asked her to keep me company. She curled up on my bed, purring contentedly. I left my bedroom door open and during the night, Dante jumped up. He cuddled close to Rosie and she did not hiss or spit at him. The next morning, I was not feeling well, so I went back to bed and rested. Rosie was with me. I told her that I loved spending time with her and she was welcome to keep me company whenever she felt lonely.

I explained to her that her young cats would still need her and they loved her very much. From that day on, Rosie has never hissed at or shown aggression toward her offspring.

Overall we continue to derive enormous joy and satisfaction from observing and participating in the interaction and diversity of the multifaceted relationships in our animal sanctuary.

Chapter Three

Healing

SINCE writing *What the Animals Tell Me*, I have received letters from people all over the world asking if it is possible for them to learn how to heal. The answer is yes.

To become a healer a person must have great love and compassion and a willingness to trust their imagination coupled with the development of positive mental discipline. By carefully channeling thoughts, you will realize you can go beyond the limits of your body. Your first step toward becoming a healer is learning to think positively. Negativity is like a disease, an easily acquired bad habit that changes your energy. When you think negatively, energy is drawn into your brain causing congestion, leading to problems in the physical body. Each negative thought must be replaced by a positive one.

Thinking positively expands mind energy outward. Positive flow releases congestion from the brain cells. By thinking positively, your physical body will become healthier, your mind will sharpen, and your confidence will increase. You will experience joy as you discover you can change the energy around you. Soon, thinking positively will become routine and as you progress with your healing skills, you will experience different levels of consciousness. You have begun your spiritual journey.

In becoming more enlightened, you will regain connection to your spiritual self. As you begin to expand your mind, you will begin to feel and sense your spirit guides. They will be with you as you face new challenges, discover new ideas, and explore new perceptions. You will experience the connection between mind, body, and spirit.

Many of the people I speak to when I conduct seminars—or in the course of my daily life and work—think of themselves as simple physical forms. Later in this book you will find exercises designed to sharpen your awareness, expand your mind, and teach you to trust your impressions while also learning to recognize your spirit guides. You will soon understand you are very much more than just a physical being.

As you allow your imagination to expand, your heart and mind will begin to open. The feelings and emotions you experience will be unique to you since each person's imagination is different.

Life Force

We are surrounded by unseen energies. For instance, you can experience an electric shock without seeing it. When the wind blows on your face or hair, you can't see it but you can feel it. Healers see and feel "unseen" energy systems and use them. Energy is the life force of the universe. It flows around us and through us. Our bodies are energy arranged in solid forms.

Healing is the transmission of energy—invisible power that occupies the physical body and extends beyond the body.

Healing Exercises to Expand Your Awareness and Senses

EXERCISE 1

Here are some exercises you can practice as you go about daily life. They will heighten your awareness of the energy fields and as your awareness becomes keener, you will notice a difference in the atmospheres of places you visit.

When you are in a restaurant, close your eyes and tune in to your emotional body to sense and feel the energy around you. Be aware of the feelings and sensations. The next time you visit the supermarket, do the same. Stop, close your eyes, and use your emotional and intuitive body to test the energy surrounding you. The more you tune in to your feelings, emotions, and senses, the more you will begin to sense the differences in the energy fields near you.

The energy in a restaurant, theater, or supermarket is very different from the peaceful atmosphere of a church. In learning to identify the difference in feeling and sensing energy, you are expanding your intuitive senses.

By practicing the following exercises, you will be developing your awareness, learning the power of your imagination, and teaching yourself to trust them.

Meditation

EXERCISE 2

In this exercise, you will be daydreaming, projecting, and expanding your mind's energy, and going on an imaginative journey. Sit in a comfortable chair or lie on the bed. Turn off the television and telephone. Breathe deeply five times.

Now think about your favorite place—on a beach, by a river, walking through a green meadow full of colorful wildflowers. Choose somewhere that makes you feel happy and peaceful. Go to these wonderful places with your mind. Each time you do this you are expanding your mind energy outward toward the universe. Your body will relax and you will experience a feeling of floating as you allow your imagination to flow.

Journey to the True Spirit Guides

EXERCISE 3

Imagine yourself on a beach. Feel the sun on your body, the wind gently blowing through your hair. To the left you see a beautiful beach house waiting for you to enter and you wander across, climb up the steps, open the door, and walk inside. A large room with enormous glass windows overlooks the ocean where the sun is brightly shining. There is a big table with chairs around it. Sit down there.

Now visualize your guides sitting there with you. Feel peace and contentment as you sense your guides' presence. You don't have to know their names. Just know and trust them. Sit quietly. Listen with your thoughts, feelings, and senses. Perhaps you will hear your guides communicating with you telepathically, or maybe you will just feel peace and tranquility as you share the silence with them. Enjoy.

Your visualization will not be solid like a picture, more like an impression since you will be seeing with your mind's eye. Everything looks different, dreamy. You are linked with cosmic forces. You are energy, just as your guides are energy.

Now visualize one of your guides rising and holding out his hand, beckoning you to follow him. Take his hand and go with him into another room. Here are two large, comfortable armchairs. A beautiful blue mist is flowing through the room. See that mist. Sit with your guide, allowing the mist to infuse you. Feel peace and tranquility throughout your body.

Later your guide once again holds out his hand and leads you into another room where the center is piled with cushions. Sit there silently with your guides. This is a special room where you are absorbing knowledge telepathically from your guides. You will have a feeling of total peace and happiness. Look around, aware that you are absorbing knowledge. Don't expect this to be instantly clear. You are being given wisdom that will manifest itself later, when you need to use it.

Again, your guide holds out his hand and leads you to another room where you sit quietly and look around. Do you see or feel a familiar animal? Is there a feline of yours that has entered this dimension? If you see or feel his presence, talk to him, mentally feeling your energy link with his. You'll be aware of other animals that have passed on to the spirit world.

Look around for any other loved ones who have left the earth plane. Feel the love and peace around you and take in the energy of this wonderful place. After a while, your guides will lead you back toward the beach. With your energized mind, create a comfortable chair and feel yourself resting on it. As you start to descend from your astral journey, you will become aware of your physical body growing heavier.

You have returned from your journey. Imagine walking from the beach and driving home. Your creative imagination has taken you on this trip. Keep practicing the exercise and trust that your spirit guides are there with you. Don't stop talking to them because you're not sure they are still with you; they are, and have been since you returned to a physical body. Speak telepathically to your guides. Listen to their replies.

If you want to name your guides, do, or ask for their names. If you receive a telepathic answer, use that name. Otherwise guides will be happy with any names you choose. They are always joyful when you acknowledge and accept them. Remember that they have been in the human form, lived on the physical plane, and understand the human world.

Mind Energy Healing Exercises

EXERCISE 4

All the exercises we've discussed and practiced up to this point are necessary to help you activate your imagination and your awareness of the energy fields surrounding you.

The next exercise will lead directly into the actual healing process, but first let me explain the different types of healing. When using hands-on healing, energy is manipulated by touch or by the healer being very near the patient. In mind-energy healing, the healer uses his or her ability to tap in to the constant flow of universal energy in order to help the patient, without actually touching him.

Let's begin by learning how to use mind-energy healing.

While in a meditative state, imagine a huge crystal-clear glass tank (similar to a large fish aquarium) filled with absolutely clear water. Visualize beautiful crystals of all sizes and shapes lying on the bottom. Look at the crystals and see them vibrating colors. The colors are powerful healing energies that penetrate the white sterilizing water. Visualize healing angels around the tank and a beautiful white light surrounding them. Watch the spiritual light shining through the water.

Imagine your cat diving into this beautiful crystal tank with color rays vibrating through the white spiritual water. He is swimming up and down, enjoying the new experience. See this beautiful white healing liquid soak into his skin, then into his bones. Imagine the liquid purifying his blood as it soaks into all the bodily tissues.

Visualize your feline's skin, bones, muscle tissues, blood, heart, lungs, liver, kidney, bladder, urinary tract, intestines, womb, stomach, cell tissues, and all other organs. Imagine the body completely soaked in the healing liquids.

After a time, you will start to see energy being released from his physical body. Everyone sees this energy differently. To me, it resembles smoke rising from a fire. It may be either a dark or light-colored smoke. Your perception of this dark energy dissipating into the water may be different. Whatever you see, your visualization will be right.

When we see the darker energy dispersing into the white liquid, give that dark energy over to the Holy Spirit as this is diseased energy being released from the body. See this darker energy flow to the top of the tank. Ask the Holy Spirit to take care of it. The darker energy will disappear.

To finish the healing session, visualize your cat floating to the top of the tank. See the angels lift him out onto a beautiful white pillow and know that your mental visualization and healing energy have been successful.

As you progress further with your healing abilities, you will begin to see colors in your imagination and your mind's eye. All colors are healing energies. As you become more adept at healing, your spirit guides will beam down the colors you need for individual healing sessions.

Pay special attention to the part of the physical body that is sick. For example, if your cat has a urinary tract infection, concentrate there. While the cat is still in your imaginary crystal tank, and after using the white liquid as a sterilizing light force through all the organs, come back to the unwell part of the body and concentrate on it. Visualize a blue light, first soaking into the whole body then into the ailing part. Now visualize this part being healthy.

Your mind energy is powerful. Be positive in your thoughts and your efforts will be rewarded. Know that your mind power has been successful. Concentration combined with visualization and complete relaxation is the key.

By using the exercises I've just outlined, you have been expanding your imagination and mind energy. Trust your impressions and be patient. You have started disciplining the power of your mind and thoughts and becoming independent. Make up your mind that you can heal. I know you can do it.

Hands-on Healing

When I am using hands-on healing, I am aware of my spiritual guides. I trust my clairvoyant impressions completely. A spirit guide beams down the colors to use when I'm healing. I see the colors I need.

When you use your hands for healing your cat, you are transferring energy into the feline's body. The energy you transmit opens up energy channels in the feline's body. When the cat is sick or an internal organ is troubled, energy is blocked. The transfer of healing energy opens up the channels so congestion can be freed. Often illness appears in a different location from the blockage. However, once you start healing with your hands, this frees the blockages and helps energy flow throughout the physical form.

It may take a few hours for the results of the energy you transferred to become apparent since it takes time for energy to infuse the system. Fortunately, the body is an incredible machine, capable of repairing itself. Once the congested energy causing the physical problem starts to flow, the body is able to heal itself and recovery begins.

You can never over-heal, so continue your healing as you sense it is necessary, on a daily basis. Continue to use your hands-on healing after the feline is well because you'll be keeping all the energy lines open, and helping the body maintain good health.

An abundance of love and compassion is needed to heal. The love you feel as you heal with your hands or your mind energy is transmitted through you. This love energy is felt by the patient and contributes another facet to the healing process.

We all perceive energy and the colors of energy differently. Because my perception of energy is different from yours doesn't make mine right or yours wrong. The way you perceive energy is right for you, just as the way I perceive it is right for me. Always trust what you feel, sense, and see.

Everyone's experience is unique. By following these simple exercises and understanding how energy waves work, you can enhance your life and the lives of your animal friends.

This applies especially to cats, who have a natural ability to plug in to mind energy. When you begin using healing energy, your feline companion will start to listen. Soon you'll learn to project more and more with your mind. Eventually, this will become second nature. Never be fearful about using your healing skills. Fear can imprison the mind and destroy your ability. There is nothing magical or supernatural about using natural abilities to help others. The only bad thing connected with healing is not making the most of those abilities.

Healing with Color

After you have practiced visualizing your cat bathed in a healing white light, you will want to continue improving your skills by moving on to other colors that can expand your healing abilities.

Blue and purple are wonderful healing colors. As you continue healing, some of you will see colors more easily than other people. If a color doesn't appear to you when you are practicing, then imagine blue or purple. However, as you begin your session, always start with white, the sterilizing color, then move on to the other colors.

Let's start practicing using your mind energy to perceive or imagine other healing colors.

Look into the crystal tank and see the water. Does the water appear to be another color? If it's green, then continue to visualize it as green. Or you may see tones of orange, red, purple, blue, gold, silver, or other colors. If you do, continue to imagine this color in the healing water. If you see two colors, then use both. Remember, whatever you perceive is right for you.

The main thing is to continue visualizing and concentrating on that color. If you are not able to see any color, try to imagine blue.

Let's say you see blue in the crystal tank. See your cat diving back into this blue water and swimming up and down. Visualize the blue water being absorbed into all the cells and tissues. If there is any residue of dark leaving the body and rising to the top of the tank, give that over to the Holy Spirit to convert or ask your guides to convert the energy to a higher level of the universe.

See and imagine blue absorbed by the organs just as you did white. Again, concentrate on the part of the body that is sick. Now your feline patient has white and blue all through his body.

Begin to visualize or imagine pink in the crystal tank. If you have seen and are using other colors, follow the same steps for each color, always saving pink for last—it is an antiseptic and soothing color. See pink penetrate the whole body. Afterward, see your cat swimming to the top of the tank with healing angels lifting him out onto a soft blanket, leaving him to rest and recover. Finally, open your eyes.

Practice these exercises regularly and you will find how easy they become. You cannot do harm when you are healing. You can never make a mistake.

Healing Color Table

Pink: Soothing. Use as an antiseptic; calming.

Green: Calming. Use for nervous tension, headaches, muscle spasms, adrenal glands and acidity.

Yellow: Good for purifying.

Gold: Very spiritual. Calming.

Blue: Peaceful. Can be used for depression, inflammation, calming. You can use blue for any ailment.

Purple: Very powerful. Helps with all disease. A spiritual color with special healing energy.

White: Used for sterilizing and protection.

Red: Good for reducing the pain of arthritis and inflammation, breaking up calcium deposits, and to give strength.

Violet: For emotional problems, nerves, and fatigue.

When you are healing, don't be concerned about perceiving the correct color. You will attract the color that is needed while you are healing. You will see it in your mind's eye but if you don't, ask your spirit guide for the correct color. The colors will become clearer the longer you work with them. Color is a cosmic energy, a spiritual force. You are joining up with this force when you encounter rays of color.

Assuming your vet has already diagnosed the problem with your cat and you're following his or her advice, you can help your pet by following the healing exercises I've explained. They will enhance the healing process and are sometimes capable of healing by themselves. But before using these exercises on humans or animals, you must first always ask their permission.

Rusty and Ernie

My clients Marie and James are a wonderful couple who live with their three cats Rusty, Xena, and Ernie and their three dogs, Casey, Shadow, and Jax. They came to me so I could speak to their animal family, and in my dealings with them I found that the advice of my own main spirit guide, Dr. David Thompson, was hugely helpful. Readers of my first book will find a full description of this wonderful influence in the chapter called *Healing with the Angels*.

That day, Rusty had not been feeling well and Marie wanted me to use hands-on healing to help him. As I tuned in to Rusty, he started to tell me about his symptoms. I told Marie and James how Rusty felt. Rusty was now fourteen years old and his physical body was beginning to wear out. He informed me he was not going to the vet again. Few cats like to visit the vet. I informed Rusty the vet was there to help him, and even humans had to visit their doctors. Marie and James laughed.

I worked on Rusty by putting my hands on his body. As I transmitted the energy, I felt it working on Rusty's kidneys.

Healing works on the energy counterparts, and I could see the congested energy around the kidneys. As the transference continued, I could feel the channels in Rusty's body opening, allowing the removal of congested energy.

Rusty was a very good patient and stayed relaxed and happy as he lay on his blanket. I thanked him for coming, and then I began talking to the rest of Marie and James's animal family.

When I tuned in to Ernie I began feeling very lethargic. My body felt quite thin, and I seemed to have lost my appetite. I asked how long ago Ernie had been losing weight and Marie said he had stopped eating well when he started having weekly injections. She was worried about this. I thanked Ernie for telling me how he felt. He said he did not want to have the injections anymore. Marie explained the vet said he would have to continue weekly shots for the rest of his life. Marie was not any happier about this prospect than Ernie. She went on to say Ernie's coat was dull, he had very little energy, and spent most of the day sleeping. She felt his quality of life was poor.

I could feel there was a problem with his blood and his immune system was beginning to break down. Marie said that Ernie had been diagnosed as having the cat form of AIDS. I told her that master herbalist Joel Hyman in California could recommend a course of herbs to clean his blood and, once the herbs had done their work, there was a chance Ernie could be cured.

I explained I was a great believer in herbs since many cats had responded extremely well to herbal treatments. Moreover, a few months earlier, I had arthritis, but after taking herbs from Joel for three months and changing my diet as he recommended, I had no more dull aches in my bones. Marie and James decided to contact Joel.

Several months later, Marie and James had another appointment with me for a healing session with Rusty, and for me to talk to their other furry companions. Both cats were very happy. Ernie was now completely cured of his blood virus. He was energetic, had put on weight and his coat was shining. He was as fit as he had been before he started having the course of injections. He had taken Joel's herbs three times a day for three months.

The herb-taking procedure had been made easier by Marie's use of two syringes without their needles. She filled one syringe with chicken jelly from a roast and the other with honey water with herbs in it. She would scoop up the brown jelly from the roasting pan and chill it. Just before mixing the herbs for Ernie, she would melt the chicken jelly in a small pan then fill one syringe with the delicious, lukewarm jelly and the second syringe with the herbal remedy. She put some of the chicken jelly into Ernie's mouth and he would lap up the juice. Then she would quickly put the other syringe with the herbal mixture into his mouth and then finish with the chicken juice. That way Ernie didn't mind the flavor of the herbs as much since their bitterness was quickly replaced by the delicious chicken jelly.

I am finding myself moving more and more toward alternative medicines like herbs and acupuncture. Animals seem to respond well to acupuncture because they have a similar network of energy lines and reflex points as the human body. Acupuncture increases circulation and releases endorphins, the body's natural pain relievers. Additionally, acupuncture decreases in-flammation externally and internally.

But sometimes herbs, healing, acupuncture, or medicine from a vet can't cure the problem. That's when it's time to let go.

When to Say Goodbye

If it's time for your animal to leave his physical body, then give him your blessing. Even though you may not want your pet to leave you, it just might be his time to go.

Death is a natural part of life and animals do not share our fear of it. They do worry about the pain they cause their human companions when they depart. Saying goodbye to your cat will be painful, but if he is suffering, it is time to let go. You will miss the comfort of his physical presence. You may feel lonely and you will never get over his leaving his physical body, but you will, in time, get used to living without him.

If you understand your cat is going to a wonderful place and will no longer be in pain, perhaps you can be happy for him.

There are times when we pray to God and His answer is not the answer we really wanted. However, we must accept it. The same goes for your pet. If it is his time to go, accept it. Help your pet by telling him that it's okay to leave.

$\mathcal{S}$ebastian

Always ask the animal's permission before you begin healing. In all the time I've been healing, only one animal has ever refused me. This extraordinary feline's name was Sebastian.

He and his human companion, Anna, lived in Kent. Anna is extremely clairvoyant. She and Sebastian shared their lives for twelve years. Before living with Anna, Sebastian had lived with a young woman who left him alone for long periods while she traveled with her work. Although she made arrangements for someone to come in and feed him, Sebastian was not happy.

One day he decided to find a new home. He had a cat door so he was able to come and go as he pleased. He wanted to live with a human who would be there for him, as he was becoming lonely and depressed spending so much time on his own.

During the day, he would investigate locally. Part of his territory included a beautiful small Tudor-style house and a garden that was a cat's paradise, full of overgrown hedges, shrubs and flowers. Much to Sebastian's delight, the garden was occupied by many small creatures, including voles, mice, birds, rabbits, and the occasional rat. He loved this garden. The scents of the animals excited him. He was also aware of the distant smell of another cat who had once inhabited this territory. Occasionally he spotted a spirit cat and knew this garden had been the cat's home when he was in his physical body.

Early one morning Sebastian saw the spirit cat sitting on an old wooden bench looking at him. The spirit cat began communicating with him. He told Sebastian he knew he was sad and said he could help him find a perfect human companion to live with. He said his friend Anna was quite lonely since he had passed into the spirit world and would welcome Sebastian and give him the home he had always dreamed about.

All Sebastian had to do was to jump on the bench and join him. When Sebastian did so, the spirit cat told him to look toward the window because his friend Anna always looked out at the bench each morning when she made her coffee. "That's all you have to do," the spirit cat said. He then disappeared, leaving Sebastian on the old wooden bench alone.

Anna awoke early that morning. After she pulled on her dressing gown, she drew back the curtains from the bedroom window. The morning sun shone through the trees and shimmered on a blanket of frost covering the ground. She went down the oak staircase to the kitchen below. As she was making her coffee, she glanced up, looking out the window. She immediately saw her visitor, a beautiful grey cat sitting on the bench in the same spot where her beloved cat Hector had often sat before his death. She immediately opened the kitchen door, whereupon Sebastian jumped down and strutted into the warm kitchen. From there, he walked through the rest of the house, checking out each room.

Then, meowing, he jumped on the antique Chesterfield sofa and curled up in the same spot Hector had always favored. Purring contentedly, Sebastian fell asleep, knowing he had found a new home. Anna knows nothing happens by chance and she realized her new companion was there to stay.

She understood Hector had brought this wonderful spirit into her life.

Sometime later, Anna called from England and asked me to do healing on Sebastian. He had kidney problems and had become quite ill. This often happens in older cats. I tuned in to Sebastian and started to speak to him.

He told me his work was over here and he would be leaving his physical body in a few days. He and Anna had shared a wonderful life together. Sebastian helped Anna in her clairvoyant work, particularly psychic absent healing, and had become a great healer himself. His body was deteriorating. He had kidney and lung problems and a tumor. He wanted to leave his physical body and journey into the spirit world.

Anna was so distressed over Sebastian's leaving she was unable to communicate with him, much less to heal him. I told her it was his time to go and he would like to have her permission to leave his physical body. Anna knew it was time to let Sebastian go but found this very difficult.

But as he requested, she gave Sebastian her love and told him it was okay to leave. She did not want him to hang on to life, because she knew he was in pain and it would have been wrong to expect him to remain any longer in his worn-out physical body. She also knew when her time came she would be journeying on to a higher dimension and would be reunited with Sebastian. She also knew he would come back in his spirit form to visit her.

Anna planned for the vet to come to her home because she did not want Sebastian to endure going to the animal hospital. Sebastian was in his home with Anna by his side when he left his physical body. Anna felt him leave and was glad he was no longer in pain. She felt tremendous sadness, but she knew her mother and all her other friends in spirit would be waiting to greet Sebastian with great joy on the other side.

Anna will have to learn to live without Sebastian's physical form, but she can feel and sense his energy around her. She will never forget Sebastian, but she will eventually get used to living without his physical body.

When We Lose a Loved One

I am unable to tell you how to make the pain go away when your cat is no longer with you, sharing your physical life. All I know is that, as time passes, you will begin to recover.

Look back with joy and be glad of the experience and love you've received by sharing your life with your animal companion. No one can ever take away memories of the happiness you have shared with your feline friend. The wonderful relationship we share with our animals can be the wealth in our lives. When you have had such a relationship—closer even than you might experience with a human—cherish every memory with gratitude.

Willie's Story

The following healing story is told in the words of Willie's human companion, Linda.

Sonya first talked to my cat, Willie, during a session with my horse, Pac Man, who suddenly stopped his barn gossip and asked Sonya to please talk to Mummy's cat, because he was driving her crazy and she was crying every night. When Sonya asked me if this were true, I admitted it was, although I was embarrassed since I'd thought no one knew.

She asked if Willie would frequently go on trips, sometimes travels extending over weeks. Again, she was right. Every night I would go out looking for him and, if he didn't come home, I would cry, because I was afraid this time he would not return. Sonya explained to Willie how this upset me, and how, by staying home, he would make his mummy feel much better. He said he would think about it.

But when I returned that night, he was sitting at the end of the driveway waiting for me. Every night since, he has been there or within five minutes of my getting home he has flown in through the cat door to let me know that he is not missing. At the time, I had no idea that this behavioral change would play a big part in saving his life.

It was a Saturday in November and I had to get up early for a horse show. I had been vaguely aware that during the night Willie had come in, jumped on the bed but had gone back out. When he wasn't there for breakfast, I called him from both the front and back doors. It was a beautiful crisp morning and although I was uneasy, I thought he'd be in by the time I showered and dressed. He wasn't.

By now my rational mind was cussing and thinking that he had disappeared on another trip despite being so good for so many months. My intuition, however, nagged that something was very wrong. I remembered Sonya had repeatedly told me to trust my intuition and I decided to go looking for Willie. I soon found him lying very still under some trees at the side of my house. His eyes were glazed, he was barely breathing, and he was icy cold.

I quickly wrapped him in a towel, jumped in my car, and drove to the emergency clinic. As I drove, I kept one hand on Willie. Several times I thought he had stopped breathing and I'd cry "Don't you die, Willie. Don't you dare die!" And he would start breathing again. By the time I reached the clinic, his temperature had dropped to ninety-six degrees and he was in shock. The technician told the vet it looked like a poisoning. She put Willie on a heating pad and started support therapy.

I could tell from her face that the prognosis was not good. There was nothing I could do and the technician suggested I leave and call after the vet had a chance to examine Willie. I managed not to fall apart until I arrived at the horse show and saw my friend Diane who was the owner of the equestrian center where I board my horse. I sobbed and told her what had happened and she led me to her house and then called Sonya. I was sure that we would need to leave a message and she would get back to me as soon as possible. I was, therefore, shocked when she answered the phone and told Diane that she had just been talking about her, and St. Francis had visited her that morning. When she asked why he was there, he had told her she would find out. This was an answer to my prayers.

With the help of her guides, Sonya quickly saw the poison spreading in Willie's system, getting in his liver and other organs. Sonya physically became very cold and felt the distress in his throat and stomach. She knew he was gravely ill and told me that before she could do any healing, she had to ask his permission and find out if he wanted to stay or was ready to go. It was an agonizing minute while he thought about it, but finally Willie decided he would like to stay.

We spent the next forty-five minutes performing healing, with Sonya giving me a crash course. We frequently had to send "shocks" to get Willie's system to wake up and specifically to keep his heart going. We called upon our guides to help us as we visualized the healing colors flowing through his body and damaged organs. Before we hung up, Sonya told me to keep visualizing the healing and she would continue working on him.

When I called the vet he was not optimistic, since the blood work showed severe liver damage and Willie was still comatose. Over the next four days, there was little change in Willie's condition. I visited when possible and each time it broke my heart to see him with all the IVs and no interest in me or anything else. Willie had always been a strong-willed, opinionated cat and a staunch friend. We had been through bad times together and he had made some unbearable times bearable. To see him so weak was just not right.

By Wednesday the vets were beginning to suggest that he might not get better and this was prolonging the agony. I kept praying and visualizing. Thursday morning the vet called me at work and told me that if there was no change in the next four hours it would be time to make a decision to let him go.

I spoke to no one about this because I knew if I did I would cry uncontrollably. I tried to work but actually spent those four hours staring out the window of my office remembering Willie—his bossiness, his love—and wondering how I would ever fill the empty space inside if he should leave too soon.

At the appointed time, the receptionist called and asked me to hold on since the vet needed to speak to me. I thought for sure Willie was gone and was preparing myself when the vet told me that just a few minutes ago, Willie had sat up, starting talking to him, and demanded food. Furthermore, his liver functions appeared normal. To sum it up, Willie was fine and could go home. It was almost too much for me to handle. How could he be dying one minute and the next be fine? Not trusting his turnaround, I asked the vet to keep him one more night just to be sure.

I went to the barn where Diane was setting up for a clinic. I finally got the chance to ask her the question that had been nagging me since I talked to the vet. Had she talked to Sonya today? Diane said she had forgotten to tell me that Sonya had called a couple of hours ago and said she had had to do some major healing on Willie that afternoon.

Now, I take nothing away from the vets and the assistants that worked on Willie. They did a magnificent job. But sometimes we need a little miracle. There is no doubt in my mind that something wonderful and special happened to save Willie's life.

I have, since that time, used my guides and the healing lights in other situations. In particular last April, my sixteen-year-old cat, Samantha, was diagnosed with terminal cancer and given forty-eight hours to live. I could not bring myself to put her to sleep. The kind vet told me to take her home for the weekend and make peace with it. That was eight months ago and she's still going strong.

Thanks.

Linda Graham, December 2000

Companion Animals

We have been discussing healing and our ability to transfer and use energy. But there is another aspect of healing associated with cats and other companion animals that is only now being explored by the medical community.

It is in the area termed *companion animals*.

It is no surprise to me that the benefits that humans derive from living with and loving animals are finally being studied. At a recent Society for Companion Animal Studies seminar held at Guy's Hospital, London, and reported in its journal, Professor Sam Ahmedzai, Professor of Palliative Medicine at Sheffield University Medical School, suggested the potential health benefits of owning or having access to pets are being underexploited.

He noted a study that demonstrated reduced blood pressure, increased levels of phenylethlamine and endorphins (the body's mood-enhancing and pain-relieving chemicals), and decreasing levels of cortisol, a substance associated with stress, in subjects who stroked their pets (in this case, dogs).

He went on to say there were other studies showing how human-pet interaction favorably impacts on blood lipids, glucose, and thrombotic factors as well as influencing the body's own production of substances that boost the immune system, relieve pain, and generate a sense of well-being.

Studies in Australia have noted beneficial effects on one-year survival rates following heart attacks and improved heart rates and blood pressure of humans with regular contact with pets. Other studies suggest pet owners consult GPs less frequently and require fewer hospital services.

As early as the 1960s, the late Dr. Boris Levinson, practicing in New York, found the presence of a pet during psychiatric sessions greatly improved contact with his patients. He went on to write about the emotional and educational benefits of pet ownership.

Since that time, cats and dogs have been used in nursing homes for elderly people to improve their quality of life. Animals have also been shown to be beneficial in the rehabilitation of prisoners. Animals help to socialize people with behavioral problems and bring pleasure and companionship to patients with chronic disease who may be isolated, disabled, or unable to communicate.

Dr. Ahmedzai and the SCAS are calling for more studies to help determine how important animals are to people's health and how pets can be better utilized in a medical setting.

I've known most of this all my life.

It's the unconditional love they give us humans, and the emotional support they are able to project that provide these benefits to human health. If you're a cat lover, no one needs to convince you how important your cat is to your health. Just being in his presence brings joy, happiness, and laughter. When we feel love for our cats, our body and organs relax. The simple act of touching and stroking our felines is therapeutic. The loyal affection we receive from them is a form of healing energy.

You don't need special knowledge to become a healer. You may even think, "I'm sure I'm not one." But each time you feel the infinite love you have for your feline vibrating through your body and your home, you are projecting healing energy. Your telepathic energy is a positive force through which you are helping to send healing throughout the universe.

Each day we share with our animal companions enriches our lives. As we experience the pure love they project to us, we are more able to heal ourselves and others.

How wise the Beatles were in the sixties to understand that "All You Need Is Love." It is through the universal energy fields, fueled by love, that miracles are performed.

Chapter Four

The Happy Cat

I find there are more happy cats than problem cats—perhaps because cats have some special abilities they can use when they need entertainment or perhaps because cats are so good at training their human companions!

One of the most fascinating things about cats is the diversity of their personalities, just like humans. They all have different ways of facing life, just as humans do and have their own ways to keep themselves amused. The idea that your cat can tune in to your thoughts and conversations at any time may be disconcerting to some cat lovers, but the idea that he can entertain himself while you're away by tuning in to your activities is probably just intriguing.

Most cats keep the telepathic lines with their

human companions open. Many tune in to the energy fields and are easily able to pick up the mind energy their human companions are constantly transmitting. You already have an energy link with your cat because you have lived together and established a pattern of communication. You probably delight in watching your cat's antics and telling your friends entertaining stories about them. Your cat may well tune in to the telepathic energy line connecting the two of you and listen in on these conversations. This helps to keep him entertained as well as helping to make him feel happy as he receives the love you transmit.

I decided to ask my friend Ann's cat how he spends his day while she is at work. Hubert said he would be delighted to tell me how he spends the day and I have put into my own words what he said.

I have lived all my life in this apartment. My day is spent on my own. I like it like that.

Once my mother brought home another cat. I was disgusted. She thought the cat would be company for me, but he had no manners and ate from my dish. I ran him off and spat at him.

I did not speak to her for a while. I was very annoyed. Finally she gave him to her sister. He is now happy living with two other cats. I was pleased to have my apartment back to myself. I love spending the day alone. I take care of the apartment while my mum is at work. I have plenty to eat and all the food is mine. I can eat as much as I like, and I don't have to share with other cats.

I have trouble with my joints. They are often stiff, but I still jump pretty well. Before my human leaves for work, she always comes to me and asks me to take care of the place while she's away. And I do, as we are best friends. She adores me. She thinks and talks about me frequently during her working day. I like to listen to her thoughts.

Sometimes I'm very nervous, and I don't know why. Those days I hide under the bed. All my toys are there, and sometimes I play with them. I like to drink from the bathroom tap, so Mum leaves it dripping. I often splash in the water with my paws.

Sometimes Mum leaves her slippers in the kitchen. She knows that I like to bite them and play with them. During the day I check out the apartment. I get into all the closets. I can open the doors with my claws. Mum tells everyone how clever I am. She leaves the bed unmade because I like to curl up on the blue sheets—they're my favorite color—and go to sleep smelling my mum's scent. That makes me happy.

Sometimes a spirit cat comes to see me. He tells me he lived in my apartment before I did. I play with him and he doesn't eat my food. He's my friend. I like him very much, but he doesn't stay long, just pops in to see me. He died from old age. He told me he lived to be seventeen and that his body would no longer work for him. He was pleased to go to the spirit world. When I chase him at night, my human companion is puzzled because she can't see my spirit friend and wonders what I'm chasing through the rooms.

If the sun is shining, I lie by the window and look out. I watch birds flying. I've always lived inside, and I'm definitely a house cat. I like living the life of an indoor cat. I sometimes see a cat that lives outside and communicates with me. He sits on a wall and tells me he can catch birds and he's a good hunter. He seems very proud of that. I'm pleased I don't have to hunt for my food. He also informs me he's a very good fighter. He likes me, but thinks it's strange I live inside all day. I tell him I am very happy like this.

What I look forward to the most is my human companion coming home. We're always happy to see each other, and she often brings me something nice to eat. In the evenings we cuddle up together on the sofa and watch TV. When there are animals on the screen, I go very close to the TV and try to catch them.

My companion will often have a snack in the evening. She allows me to lick the butter from the toast. I curl up on her hair and sometimes play with it. The scent and feel of her hair reminds me of another cat. Then we fall asleep together.

My human companion thinks her life is boring, but we both love our lives the way they are. She often informs me she would rather share her life with me than any man, and I agree with her. I am a very happy cat.

Now that you've heard Hubert's story, I'll tell you some stories of other happy cats. Some have not always been happy but when changes for the better have been made in their lives, their behavior and personalities blossomed.

Patrick and Sophie

My son Patrick and his friends Anna and Simon had just moved into an Edwardian house in London when he heard about a cat needing a home. The cat had been living with her human companions for ten years but they were moving to Australia and, since she was quite nervous, they felt the journey would be terrifying for her. Finding her a suitable home seemed the best solution.

Like children, cats require a commitment of time and care. Patrick was well aware of this. He knew Sophie might have trouble adapting to a new environment, especially since she was shy and had never moved before. On top of that, she would be losing her old human family and gaining three strange new human companions. Patrick was born exuding great happiness. He possesses an abundance of compassion and love and a sense of humor that lifts your spirit. Wherever Patrick is, you hear laughter. I knew if anyone could bring happiness and confidence to a shy feline, it was he.

Sophie's human family said she was nervous and was constantly being attacked by other neighborhood cats, and that she also spent most of her time in the house hiding in a cupboard or under a bed. Patrick had his work cut out.

When Sophie arrived, Patrick was well-equipped with cat dishes, litter tray, etc. and knew she would have to be kept indoors for at least three weeks. After her human companions left, Sophie crept under the sofa and there she stayed, during the day, for the next three weeks. At night she'd investigate her new environment, but whenever anyone entered the room, she retreated under the sofa.

Patrick, Simon, and Anna all loved their shy new feline friend and wanted to see more of her. During the next three weeks, each time I talked to Patrick, the whole conversation revolved around Sophie. I'd talked to Sophie, too, explaining why she had a new home. She seemed to understand.

After four weeks, Patrick decided it was time for Sophie to be more sociable. Armed with a special "cat fishing pole" with a fish on the end, he enticed Sophie out and told her he wanted her to be a happy, contented cat from now on. He picked her up and put her in the garden, leaving the door open, telling her she was now allowed to go outside. He also told her he wasn't good at emptying litter boxes and found the whole thing distasteful, so could she go outside in future?

Sophie started to use the garden for her business, as she had during her former life. Each day Patrick would put her in the garden, leaving the kitchen door open for her to come back in when she was ready, but telling her firmly that she must lead a happy cat's life and that he would help her. He told her if any cats came in the garden, she was to chase them off. He'd help her if necessary. But she was not allowed to disappear under the sofa every time she came into the house as he wanted her for a companion and Anna and Simon wanted to see her beautiful face and lovely body sitting on the sofa, not hiding underneath it. He told her happy, contented cats did not hide all the time. Sophie always listened to him intently.

I talked to Sophie one Sunday while I was speaking with Patrick on the phone and explained that it was okay for her to use all of the house. She told me her other human companions had just accepted her hiding all the time. I said Patrick needed her to take care of the house while he was working. That was her work.

Cats love to have a job to do. At last she had a purpose.

Each day, as Patrick left for work, he got down on the floor close to Sophie, looked in her eyes and told her he was leaving and would be home later. Gradually, Sophie got more adventurous and began to lie on the sofa. One day Simon came home and found her on his bed. She was beginning to socialize but she continued to avoid Anna's room. Patrick phoned me to ask why.

When I communicated with Sophie, she told me Anna's bedroom "stinks." Patrick confirmed Anna used a strong perfume and Sophie was quite right! Sophie went on to tell me the smell made her nostrils sting. She said she liked Anna, but not her smell. Patrick was able to tell Anna why Sophie had not curled up on her bed.

As the weeks went by, Sophie's personality changed from shy and insecure to outgoing and happy. She exuded confidence. She began to chase other cats out of her garden. She had the run of the house and no longer hid when people approached.

When I speak to her, she tells me she loves all the attention she's getting and understands she's part of the family. She also tells me what she has eaten—all the best foods, from fresh salmon and tuna to butter and milk. She says she enjoys eating off people's plates. Patrick admits that, though Sophie knows she's not to jump up on countertops, he thinks she does, occasionally. She has three bedrooms, a kitchen and a cellar to look after and snuggles up at night on her human companions' beds, purring contentedly.

Sophie is constantly told how much she is loved and appreciated. She has been made to feel a part of her new human companions' family. She is told when their routine is going to change, when they will be gone, and for how long. Though it took Sophie a little time to adapt to her new environment, Patrick was determined to help her learn to enjoy her life like the special cat she is.

Cats want to please us and make us happy. It's important to communicate very clearly what we expect of them. Once we get our pets into a good routine, the rest is pure enjoyment. Gone forever is the shy, nervous Sophie and in her place is a confident, secure, relaxed, happy cat that has Anna, Simon, and Patrick wrapped firmly around her little paw.

Cinnamon and Raisin

My daughter, Emma, was about to move house. Her cats, Cinnamon and Raisin, were excited. Often cats don't like to move house, but Cinnamon and Raisin have enjoyed traveling in the car with Emma since they were very young and have moved with her several times.

However, this move was going to be different. Emma had just married and her husband, William, already had a cat. Honey had been William's companion for several years. I got quite an insight into Honey's character when I communicated with her just before the move. She did not seem upset that there would be new animals in her life. She said she missed William when he was away and would welcome company.

I asked if she would allow Emma, Cinnamon, and Raisin into her house and life. She informed me that she liked Emma but was not sure about the cats until she met them. That was a big breakthrough. Honey was willing for them to come and curious about them, but she was not prepared to greet the newcomers in an open and friendly way. It is not uncommon for cats in this situation to tolerate incomers but either to ignore them or treat them with some disdain and a kind of "keep your distance" attitude. This can sometimes be permanent. Honey, however, had a natural curiosity about the newcomers.

She informed me she knew Cinnamon and Raisin were indoor cats and that she was a clever cat because she knew how to hunt. I could feel a subdued excitement from her. She was curious about the new cats but didn't want them to eat from her dish or sleep in her bed. I told her that wouldn't happen.

Cinnamon and Raisin were used to living with other cats and dogs as they often stayed with me while Emma was away. They were excited at the thought of moving to the country and becoming outdoor cats. I explained that Honey was allowing them to live with her. All three cats were taking a practical view of the move.

I tuned in after the move to all the cats. Emma had kept Cinnamon and Raisin away from the basement where Honey spent most of her time. Most encounters between the three cats took place in the kitchen. Occasionally Honey would hiss and disappear. But gradually, all three cats accepted each other.

Honey is always there when Cinnamon and Raisin venture outside. Emma thanks Honey for helping the two new arrivals to become familiar with outdoor life. Honey watches them with interest as they explore her territory, not objecting at all. Emma continues to tell Honey she is very wise and kind to allow them all to live together. She is rewarded with fresh shrimp, turkey, and chicken and made to feel like a queen. Cinnamon and Raisin continue to enjoy being indoor/outdoor cats, and being able to venture out into their natural environment.

Tips When Moving

Moving can be a stressful time for cat companions and their felines. Remember to confine your cat in the new house for the first ten days after you move. During the day, keep him in a room with the door closed. At night you may open the door to the cat's room and leave it open until the next morning.

Your feline will feel more secure in the dark, when appliances aren't running, the TV is off, and traffic noise is less, and may well explore the rest of the house then, becoming familiar with the many different scents of his new home.

When you awaken, make sure to confine your cat to his room during the day for the first few days. After that, if you are sure no one will leave a door open to the outside, you can let him have the run of the house. After about ten days, allow your cat to find his way into the garden. Female cats need little more territory than their own yard, and many happy cats are content to stay inside a fenced garden or even indoors. However, male cats like to claim anywhere from three to twelve times as much territory. If your male cat is an outdoor cat, he will wander farther from home than his female counterpart.

If you have a male cat and are concerned for his safety, then send him a picture of the dangers that await him in the world outside his garden fence. Check chapter two for more details on how to influence your cat to stay in your yard. If your cat is an indoor cat this will not be a worry for you.

There are behavioral differences with regard to wandering and territorial aggression between male cats who are brought up as mainly outdoor animals and those who can be termed household cats. The difference will be evident but less extreme if they have been spayed.

The spayed outdoor cat will still have the urge to wander but he will generally be less aggressive and territorial and is more likely to respond to requests to come inside when called. The indoor male cat, once spayed, becomes much more relaxed and approachable but is prone to gain weight if his diet is not adjusted.

Remember that those first ten days indoors after the move are very important. It will enable your feline companion to form an energy link with his new location as well as give him time to become familiar with all the strange sights, noises, and scents the new home will present.

Sophie Elizabeth

One day I was consulted by one of my clients, Jeri, a beautiful little lady with a bright smile who is a great cat lover and the proud mum of a Persian cat called KT who was nearing the time when he would pass over to the other side.

Jeri had visited me previously to ask if KT would mind if she brought a kitten into their home. He was quite happy about having a new arrival as long as the kitten had his own dishes and his own bed, as KT had no wish to share his precious possessions with any other feline.

When Jeri arrived at my office for the consultation I was surprised that in addition to a photograph of the new arrival she had brought two other cats. She explained that Rose and Rodge belonged to her friend Sharon and that she was looking after them for a while. This was a long-standing arrangement between the two women and I found it intriguing that the cats accepted the transition from one home to another without any problems and could adjust to living together at either place. The cats clearly liked each other's company. Jeri was enthusiastic as she showed me the photographs of her new arrival, Sophie Elizabeth. As usual when Jeri arrived, her husband, who had died a few years earlier, came through from the spirit world holding their precious cat, Boots, who had also passed into the spirit world.

As I tuned in to KT, he informed me he quite liked the new arrival and was happy to have her. Jeri was glad that all the cats liked Sophie Elizabeth. She told me of Sophie's background. A

woman had found her running between the cars in a supermarket parking lot. Sophie was only three weeks old. The lady
who found her had a cat at home that had just given birth to a litter of kittens and she thought she could foster the new kitten
with her mother cat. It worked: When the lady arrived home
with the new kitten she smeared Sophie with wet fish-flavored
cat food and put her in with the other kittens and by the time the
mother cat had licked off the food from the kitten, she had
adopted Sophie as one of her own. She was a very good mother
for the foundling. Sophie became strong and healthy.

Jeri wanted to know how Sophie came to be in the parking lot.
I tuned in to Sophie who told me her mother had moved her
from where she had been born into a nearby parking lot. When
her mother left her there and went to fetch the other kitten Sophie tried to follow her but was unable to find her and when her
mother did not return Sophie was alone. I knew that the right
person found Sophie. Of all the people who were in the parking
lot that day, the person who found her had a cat with a litter of
kittens. Spirit works in wonderful ways. That little cat and the
lady were destined to meet.

And now Sophie Elizabeth is where she is supposed to be
with a wonderful lady who is already in love with her. And all the
other cats in the family have adopted her as well. She is now with
the family she came into this life to be with.

Rosie

One hot night in June my husband, Fitz, saw in the headlights from his truck a small cat. He got out and the small tabby came up to him meowing pathetically. Next morning at breakfast he related the story to me with grave concern. Like me, he has a deep love for animals, and I could tell the plight of this small creature troubled him. The following night he left the house armed with cat food, water, and dishes.

Each morning at breakfast he would tell me about the encounters he had with his new friend. He told me as soon as he turned into the driveway, she would be running toward the headlights, and how carefully he had to drive so as not to harm her. I think she used up some of her nine lives during that first week. Fitz was already becoming emotionally involved.

The following night his new feline friend did not appear. This went on for two more nights. Then, when he told me about his worries, I felt she was shut in somewhere and could not get out. Fitz became even more concerned. But just before he left that night I felt she was no longer trapped and would be waiting for him. I could feel her energy and, by this time, I was also becoming connected with her.

The next morning at breakfast Fitz was smiling. His new feline friend had been waiting for him, ravenously hungry, and could hardly wait for him to open up the can of food.

The following Saturday I communicated to her that we would be coming for her and asked how she felt about living with us and our other animals. She told me she would like it. I explained to her in her language that we would be putting a large crate on the ground and asked her if she could please go inside it. The crate was large and had a big door that would make it easy for the cat to enter. I knew a big crate would be much less forbidding, in the cat's mind, than a small one.

I was looking forward to meeting her. That evening, we packed up cat food, water, and the crate and placed a litter tray and towel on the floor inside it.

The cat was living wild in a warehouse parking area about fifteen miles away. As Fitz was driving the van, I communicated to our new feline friend that we were on our way to help her and reminded her to please go into the crate when we put it on the ground. She told me she would and that she was very hungry and very pleased that we were coming for her. I could tell the emotion of happiness was a new experience for this little creature. She had had no joy, as yet, in her young life.

I felt the pure joy emanate from her as we pulled into the parking lot. Fitz stopped the truck and climbed out. He unloaded the crate and put it on the ground, opening the door wide. We looked around for a moment and could not see her. Then suddenly she came rushing toward the headlights. I could hear her meowing loudly. Without any hesitation, she ran straight into the crate, sat down, and looked out at both of us, and told me to take her with us.

Fitz opened a can of food and gave it to her in the crate, then closed the door and loaded her gently into the back of the van. I covered the crate with a large towel to stop headlights from other traffic frightening her on the way home. She made very little sound on the journey back. That night she settled down happily in the garage with an old pillow to sleep on and additional food and water to paw. She rubbed her head on the downy pillow and stretched her thin frail body out, purring contentedly. She knew she had come home.

When we befriend an animal, we always begin by saying we'll find a good home for it. A home other than ours! But as usual, I felt myself weakening. I began wondering if we could find room for the new arrival. Since we already had five cats and seven dogs, another animal would make very little difference.

Foxy, my small schipperke dog, had been telling me she was looking forward to meeting her new companion. I'd informed all the other animals about the new arrival. When I opened the kitchen door into the garage, the new cat ran up to Foxy and rubbed against her fur. Foxy instantly had another friend. I was interested in the reaction of the other dogs when they met the new cat. Would they all react as Foxy had?

I'm always amazed how all my animals accept each other and the other rescued animals we bring into the house until we can find a good private home for them. I know how important it is that animals living together get along well. I always emphasize how much we love them, how important they are to us, and their role in our family, especially when a new animal is brought in.

This is important, as most pets fear a newcomer may oust them from their favorite places. Cats are especially afraid of this. An older pet may fear being pushed aside by a younger animal. Newcomers can alter the balance among the other animals. You must be sensitive to all your animals' feelings. If you fail to spend quality time with your older pets after a new one arrives, they will blame the new addition for the neglect, and problems will result. When you take time to ensure your older companions still feel loved and important and emphasize that the newcomer will simply make the family happier, you can stop problems before they start.

Each one of my dogs and cats was abused before he or she came to live with us, and they instinctively know when other animals have suffered. I ask them all permission to bring in a new animal and explain that, as a family, we all take care of each other.

Honey, my alpha dog (by which I mean the dog which, until challenged and ousted, is the senior animal in the pack and the one to which the others defer), takes care of the cats. She loves them. The other dogs are very respectful of newly arrived cats as they know that if a cat has been living wild, it knows how to protect itself from other animals. It takes only one swipe of a paw full of claws to remind a dog to be respectful.

Our new arrival could smell the chicken I was cutting up for the cats' breakfast, and when I put her bowl down she ate very fast. I told her, telepathically, that I had a special name for her, Rosie, and asked her if she liked it. Immediately I felt a burst of joy and approval from her. I called all the animals together and asked them what they thought of the name. They all agreed it was a good name.

This name is very important to me, as a spirit called Rosie is one of my special guides. She had suggested I use her name for this honored new feline. And that is how Rosie became an important part of our family.

Manny and Rex

There is nothing more distressing for cat owners than if serious illness strikes and they become unable to care for their companion animal. It is even worse when the diagnosis is that the condition is terminal, so that when they are hospitalized, they have to leave their faithful friend alone, relying on caring friends to call in and to feed the lonely cat. This happened with Manny and Rex, his feline companion of fourteen years.

Manny was distraught. He had shared his triumphs and tragedies with this wonderful furry friend and the thought of not waking up with Rex and sharing each day that he had left to live was heartbreaking. I first met Manny when my daughter Emma helped run a top hairdressing and beauty salon in Houston. Her great friend Donna had opened the salon and asked Emma to join her. Manny was a stylist there and pursued another profession. Weekends and evenings he was a country and western singer. I had been invited to his concerts and, with Emma and her friends from the salon, I would thoroughly enjoy an evening of country-and-western songs. He was obviously talented and his singing career was taking off.

The last time I heard Manny sing was at a yacht club on Lake Conroe at Emma's wedding. The ceremony was by the lakeside and Manny's voice echoed across the water as he sang the emotionally laden words of the song "Amazed." It was a poignant and beautiful experience as my son-in-law, William, and Emma pledged their vows under a cabana of fresh white flowers with the sun setting over the lake. The memory of that evening will stay with me for ever.

Manny wore a Stetson hat and traditional Texas western evening wear, offering a wonderful contrast to the formality of an elegant English-American wedding with black tie and evening dresses. Manny asked me after dinner if I could talk to Rex and tell him he would not be home until late and that he was sorry that he had not been able to get back to see him during the day. I would often talk to Rex, who was a very calm and chatty cat, whenever I had my hair styled at the salon. Manny loved his feline companion very much and all the stylists would gather to hear what Rex had to tell me and enjoyed the conversation.

Soon after the wedding, Manny was diagnosed with a terminal illness and was hospitalized. He was deeply concerned about the welfare of his constant companion, who had to be left in his apartment with friends feeding him and changing his litter box. Because of the seriousness of his condition, Manny's family flew in from El Paso to be at his bedside. Emma also flew in from her home in Kansas. Emotionally and physically exhausted, Manny agonized over whether he should have Rex put down. Manny thought that this way it would be kinder to Rex than for the cat to have to go to another home and learn to live without him.

Emma rang me about Manny's dilemma. The following day she and I went to visit him in the hospital. His condition had stabilized and his family had decided that they would like to move

him back to El Paso. Manny was happy at the thought of returning to his childhood home so that he could be in a hospital close
to his family, but he was in a painful quandary as to what was the
best course to take for Rex.

As we walked into the hospital room, Manny's handsome
face lit up. He was so pleased to see us and held out his arms to
embrace Emma. Manny introduced me to his brother Bobby,
who was staying with him and going to accompany him on his
journey to El Paso. He then asked me to talk to Rex. As I tuned
in to the cat I asked him if he wanted to go to sleep and not wake
up as Manny was now very sick and would be unable to take
care of him. I also told Rex that Manny was very concerned at
the thought of him going to another home where he would be
unhappy and distressed. If he chose to go to sleep and not wake
up and journey to the wonderful spiritual realm, he would be
there to greet Manny and they could be together.

Rex thought for a moment and then asked why he could not
go with Manny to El Paso and stay with Manny's father. Then
he could visit Manny in the local hospital. This would be a good
arrangement for all. He had been to visit Manny's father before
and stayed with him at his home. He went on to say that
Manny's father was lonely sometimes and that they liked each
other.

He stressed that he was not ready to go to sleep and not wake
up. He did not want his life to come to an end, as his work on
this earth plane had not been completed.

I told Bobby and Manny how Rex felt and they agreed about
their father and Rex living together and they thought this might

work. Manny's big smile flashed across his face as they decided on this solution. As Rex received the information, he was happy.

Rex had to have his injections and a health certificate before the airline would take him, so Emma offered to go and collect Rex from the apartment. She called me to see if it would be all right to bring Rex back to my home that night so that she could take him the next day to have his shots at my vet's. He would be staying with us for two days.

I was more than happy to have Rex and suggested to Emma he could sleep in the guest room with her, but I would inform my animal family that Rex would be coming into our home. All of my animal family are used to animals coming and going and were not at all upset at the thought of a guest. I told them Rex's sad story and they were all very sympathetic. They appreciated being informed about the situation and were very happy that he would be seeing his human companion again soon.

Emma left to pick up Rex. When she arrived the key did not fit because the locks had been changed. The previous week his family had packed up all Manny's belongings and furniture and put them in storage, leaving the bed and sheets on the bed for Rex and an automatic feeder with food and water. Every other day, friends would visit Rex to see that he was okay. One of the salon stylists had visited him two days before to change the litter and refill the food and water dispensers. Now Emma found a note on the door from the owner saying that she had thrown the cat out and removed the bed.

Emma was very upset and began looking and calling Rex, who had been an indoor cat for most of his life and had been thrown out of his home. While Manny believed that Rex was safe and secure in the house, he had in fact been outside with no one to feed him and had to fend for himself.

Emma can also communicate with animals and knew Rex so she began to tune in to him. She picked him up telepathically and felt he was close. She told him to come to her as she had food for him and she was going to take care of him. She felt he was over to the left of the garden. As she walked around she was transmitting telepathically. She expressed the feeling of him trusting her and she pictured him running to her. She opened a small packet of cat treats, his favorite, and called his name.

This much-loved feline came meowing and running toward her. Emma gathered him up in her arms as she flashed him a picture of tuna fish for his supper and a feeling of love. Then Emma drove home with Rex on her knee, purring and talking to her. Rex was happy to be with Emma and felt great relief that he was no longer alone. Many cats dislike riding in cars, but Rex was so relieved to be with Emma, his trusting eyes looked up into her face and soon they arrived at my home.

The next day Emma visited the vet with Rex so that he could have his shots and get his health certificate. That night Rex slept with Emma on the bed. In the morning Emma pulled into the airport and parked. Manny was there in the wheelchair. As Emma and Rex walked toward them, Rex looking through his crate, Manny looked up and tears rolled down his face as he saw his faithful companion. They were again together and on their way home.

Claire and Judy

My friend Claire and her daughter Judy live near Lake Livingston in Texas on five acres of land. They have seven dogs and two cats, and are constantly rescuing animals. One day they were visiting a store and Judy saw a pitiful bundle of orange fur under a bench. The kitten was just a few weeks old.

The shop assistant said he had been putting out food for a few days, and though the kitten toyed with the food, it was not eating. Judy and Claire rushed the kitten to the vet. After a thorough examination, he told them that the kitten was not likely to survive. However, Claire and Judy were undeterred.

Judy lived with two other cats she had rescued, Tiger and Lady, on the top floor of the house she and Claire share. Both of them are familiar with telepathic communication and realized the introduction of the new kitten could cause havoc in their normally serene households. Judy knew it was quite important that she tell Lady and Tiger about the new arrival, so they would not feel displaced. As they were driving home from the vet Judy informed the animals already in residence about things. It's so important to emphasize how much you love all your animals, especially when there's a new animal arriving.

The dogs, who live on the ground floor of the house with Claire, were also included in the decision-making process. By telepathically informing all the animals at the house about the kitten, Judy was preventing problems before they began. Judy began by transmitting mental pictures of the arrival of the kitten at their home. She also told all the other animals, how kind they were to allow this.

When they arrived, Judy made the kitten comfortable in the bathroom, as he had to be kept in a separate place in case he had any infectious diseases. This also allowed the other cats to get used to the new scent. Scent plays an important role in cats getting acquainted. It is always a smart move not to put cats that don't know each other together right away.

With Judy's love and care, the kitten gradually gained strength and recovered completely. He was given the name Phoenix as she felt he had risen from the ashes. After a few weeks, when he was pronounced healthy, Judy began to leave the bathroom door open. By this time, Tiger and Lady were familiar with Phoenix's scent. Slowly he began to explore and after a few days of hissing and spitting, Lady began warming to Phoenix.

Judy's wisdom in including all the animals in the decision about bringing the kitten home, and being especially careful to give all the cats lots of attention, prevented feelings of jealousy. Lady began to play with the kitten and, in no time, the kitten was curled up by her side, but Tiger remained aloof.

One day when I was talking to Claire on the phone, I could feel Tiger wanted to talk to me. I connected to him through Claire's energy. I congratulated him on his progress toward the new family member. He told me the kitten ran all over the place and often came up to him but that he didn't play with Phoenix and chose to ignore him. I acknowledged that was okay, but told him he could change his mind about that if he wanted to. He transmitted a picture of the kitten face-to-face with him and said he liked that.

I told Tiger he was very important to the little one and he could teach it to play. I also told Tiger he was a very wise cat. This appealed to his ego. He listened and thought. I told him how much the kitten needed him and that he could be a father to the kitten. He asked me, "What is a father?" and I explained the role of a cat "dad." How "dads" play with their kittens and take care of them. He listened and told me he would think about it. I emphasized that this was a very important role.

Claire started laughing when I explained his reaction, but I asked her to tell me when he decided to play, if he decided to play, the role of dad. Days later Phoenix had not only a new cat mother, but also a very playful cat father. Tiger takes his role very seriously and plays with the kitten all day long!

Problems can crop up when people rescue cats. Since I can put myself in the cat's place, I can usually hit upon the solution. Most problems can be solved. Often it's as simple as looking at the situation from his point of view, then letting the cat know it's all right for him to change his mind.

Keeping Felines Together

If you are looking for a new feline companion and happen to be visiting a shelter and see two cats huddled together, please understand that those two cats have bonded. They may be siblings or have become friends. Whatever the reason, cats huddled together have an attachment for each other. Put yourself in their place. Would you want to be torn away from your family or loving companion? Remember that the very fact of being in temporary shelter probably means they've already experienced trauma of some sort. Cats understand what is happening. They are heartbroken when they are separated from their companions. Like humans, they do not get over the loss of each other, they just get used to living without their close companion.

Though some cats prefer to be alone with their human companion, most enjoy having company. They love to cuddle together, play together, eat together, talk together, and groom each other. They are capable of deep love. For this kind of cat, living alone can be traumatic. After their human companion brings them home to an unfamiliar place with unfamiliar smells, these cats need a companion for comfort. The new human companion may never understand or know the grief and pain she has caused to her new feline friend.

So please spare a thought for the other cat or kitten you may be leaving behind, and think again about how you would feel if this were happening to you. As two are always more fun than one, think about sharing your life with two feline companions. You will all be so very happy together.

Chapter Five

Attitude Problems and

Disruptive Behavior

MOST domestic cats adjust well to living in a household but a few never do. These are the ones that experience emotional upsets throughout their lives, to the concern of their owners.

In these ultrasensitive cats, the sensors are even more hypersensitive, as are the nerve endings. The ultrasensitive cat has keener reactions to atmospheric changes and air currents than other felines. Such cats may spend most of their time under a bed or hiding in a dark closet. They may object to fondles or cuddles as they can feel the electrical impulses from a human body. If you approach them too quickly, this will cause the cat discomfort. It's not being unfriendly. It's just trying to protect itself from your electrical charge.

Cats know when a storm is approaching by

sensing the heightened electromagnetic fields through their nervous system. They may be dramatically affected by such atmospheric changes. The ultrasensitive cat needs understanding and special love and acceptance of this aspect of his nature. Do everything possible to provide a comforting and nonstressful environment. This may require placing his food bowl under a bed or putting his litter box in a closet, as well as respecting his reluctance to display outward signs of affection such as being picked up.

Quite often, at night when the house is still, this cat will feel safe enough to venture out to explore other areas of the home. He may even nestle close to his human companion or companions in bed. Dissent may occur between husband and wife in even the most contented households due to the presence of a territorial feline or ardent suitor—aka the family cat—vying for the nocturnal affection of one or the other.

Studies of ten thousand pet-owning households in the United States reveal that 60 percent of pets sleep on their owners' beds. The information does not differentiate between cats and dogs but it is reasonable to assume a fairly large proportion of those animals are felines who have access to the master bedroom.

Many of the feline night-visitors share the beds of single women. This is where problems can arise. The majority of young married men will not have experienced animals sharing their beds and when the female partner insists on allowing her favorite feline to share the marital bed, they are forced to adjust. The main complaint I hear from felines sharing a human's bed is that the humans move around too much, which they find annoying while they're trying to sleep!

Attitude problems or disruptive behavior may arise from the cat being ultrasensitive or from him being unceremoniously removed from the bedroom that he had trusted to be part of his domain. Many other things that can and often do lead to disruptive behavior. They include:

1. New animals coming into the home without the existing pets being properly prepared.

2. Family tensions or emotional upsets.

3. A move of house.

4. Dietary and feeding arrangement changes including changes in feeding bowls and litter boxes.

5. A drastic change in routine.

6. A family member leaving home.

7. Visitors, particularly guests, staying overnight or for several days.

8. Having a party at your home.

9. The death of a human or animal's companion.

10. An illness in an animal or human member of the family.

11. Emotional upsets with a human companion(s).

12. Buying one animal in the household a present, toy, new collar, or food treat and not getting the same for all

the animals. All animals in the family should be treated the same way.

13. If you change one cat's food (say to a slimming food for weight loss) but not the others'.

14. Family members making fun of the cat or telling him that he is ugly.

15. Paying attention to or favoring one animal in the house more than another.

The following stories show the cat's point of view. Remember it's always a cat with a human problem, not a human with a cat problem.

Star

Occasionally, I speak to a cat that has been orphaned or removed from its mother too early and has never been taught proper cat "etiquette." Sometimes this lack of education can lead to problems with humans. Such was the case with Star and her owner, Karen, who lived in Athens in April 1991.

While she was out on a sunny morning, Karen came upon a peasant woman throwing small rocks at a pipe sticking out of a wall. Karen looked up to see a tiny kitten trying to get out of the pipe. Each time the kitten put her head out, the old woman threw another stone. Karen rescued the defenseless kitten.

Tiny as she was, the kitten's first litter box was a meat-loaf tin. She was riddled with worms but with veterinary care and Karen's love, Star recovered and grew strong, and in 1995 traveled with Karen to their new home in Texas. Karen saw me on a TV show in 1999 and consulted me about a problem with Star, who would often scratch Karen and her husband, Dimitri. She didn't seem to know how to play without using her claws.

Karen and her husband were living with Karen's aunt. Star had begun scratching the furniture and, worst of all, she would attack and scratch the aunt's legs as she walked around inside her own home. When I connected with Star, I discovered a very chatty cat with a strong personality. I soon realized Star didn't know she was causing pain to her human companions when she used her claws. I explained she needed to keep her claws in when playing with Karen and Dimitri because she was hurting them. She immediately informed me she would. I told her that Karen's aunt loved her, too. Star said she lived with her grandmother, not her aunt. When I told Karen, she laughed and said, when talking to Star, they always referred to her aunt as "Grandmother."

Then I told Star she hurt her grandmother when she attacked her legs. Star became very upset and promised she would not jump on her grandmother's legs again. Within days, Star's clawing rampages had completely stopped.

Star had been very young when she left her mother and had been raised by humans. If she had been able to play with other cats and her mother as a kitten, she would have felt the pain caused by teeth and claws and would have learned to keep her claws in. This is just one of the problems that can result if a kitten is not raised in a proper cat family environment. Star was lucky to have a human companion to raise her but although Karen made Star feel loved and important, she was unable to teach her things in the same way as a cat mother.

Through my communications, Star was able to understand how her claws were causing pain to her beloved humans. Since she had always been made to feel loved and appreciated, Star was more than happy to cooperate and draw in her claws.

Playtimes are now a joy for humans and Star.

Rusty and Julie

Very rarely do I speak to a client who is insensitive and unsympathetic in their approach to their cat. However, this *can* happen and whenever I have this experience, it makes me unhappy.

Julie was upset because her cat, Rusty, had been defecating outside his litter box. As I tuned in to Rusty, he informed me there had been a house move. I felt his sadness as he told me how this move had affected him. He had been living with two human companions when he was young, but after the move, he was living in a small apartment without one of them. He told me he missed his dad very much and asked if he would ever see him again. When I asked Julie about this she told me they had divorced and no, Rusty would not see her ex-husband again.

I told Rusty this can happen with humans but his mother would always take care of him. He told me how lonely he was since the breakup and how he missed the company of his dad who had been home all day with him. Julie confirmed that her husband worked from home when they were together. I told Julie how lonely Rusty was and what a big adjustment this was for him and she explained that when she first moved to the new apartment, Rusty used his litter box all the time. He had only begun soiling the carpet in the last few months. The soiling usually occurred during the night.

Rusty had asked me if he could have a cat for a friend. Julie said, "Not while he's soiling the carpet."

I said that cats always have a very good reason for sudden changes in their behavior and that Rusty was terribly lonely. When they had first moved, Rusty said, his mum was home every evening and at weekends but now she was away some nights and sometimes didn't come home until the afternoon. Rusty said Mum had a new boyfriend and he was spending more and more time on his own, all day and often all night. I told Julie soiling at night was Rusty's way of telling her, "Please don't leave me alone. I miss you."

Julie became defensive. "Well, I am home some evenings and most of the day on Saturdays. Ask him why, when I'm home, he sits on the chair in the other room looking out the window when he could be in the chair with me, on my knee."

I told her cats are not robots and have wills of their own. He was happy when she was home with him. Just having her in the apartment was enough. He was not going to jump on her knee and stay close to her because she expected him to. Cats are independent and don't always express affection on demand, particularly after being left alone for long periods.

Julie's life had changed. She was no longer prepared to make the commitment of time and energy it takes to care for a cat properly. She was no longer a good companion to Rusty and yet she expected him to be a good companion to her in the brief time she was at home with him. I tried to explain to Julie about giving Rusty some special treat, like tuna, occasionally. He told me his food was always the same but he remembered when his dad gave him tuna and wet cat food that he liked. Now he had the same dry food all the time. Incidentally, there's a good reason for cats' common preference for tuna—given the dubious ingredients of many commercially produced cat foods, tuna is usually reliably untainted as well as tasty.

Julie replied, "Tell him I will, but not often. And please tell him, when he does use the litter box not to dig into the litter so that it goes all over the floor."

I had to tell Julie cats do scratch the litter outside of the box sometimes and as long as Rusty was using the box, that was not an issue. Cats almost always require some cleaning up. While speaking to Julie, I began to understand why Rusty had changed his habits. This was a cat with a big human problem.

I told Julie that if she were to get another cat for company for Rusty, it would help. I also suggested she spend more time at her apartment than at her boyfriend's and to make sure when her boyfriend came over to allow Rusty to sleep on the bed. (Rusty had informed me that when the boyfriend was there Julie closed the door on him so he could not sleep on the bed.)

Julie told me she would not allow this. I reminded her she had consulted me to help with a problem, and I had to say that she was the problem, not the cat. Unless she started to understand things from Rusty's point of view, the problem would not be solved. I also reminded her of the importance of showing love to her cat every day because Rusty was starved of human affection.

Most clients will immediately understand their cat's plight and are only too pleased to make whatever changes they can. They don't continue to blame the cat once they understand its point of view. When I have a client who will not make changes and won't try to understand their cat, the problems will continue.

Tom

Susan came to see me because her male cat, Tom, was biting and spraying and had been for the entire seven years she had been married. She and her husband have two small sons. She and Tom had been together since he was a kitten. Never in the five years together before her marriage had Tom misbehaved.

When I connected telepathically with Tom, I found him greatly distressed because the man he lived with (Susan's husband) did not like cats and wanted him killed.

Susan was terribly worried about her Tom, knowing that her husband did not like cats. I told her Tom was misbehaving because his life had been turned upside down. He had been happy and secure, knowing only love during their first five years alone together. Tom told me he had moved houses many times. Susan said her husband was in the army and they had to move often.

This had been disturbing for Tom. Furthermore, Susan explained, carpeting had needed to be replaced in several houses because Tom had urinated and chewed on it. This had cost thousands of dollars and her husband repeated that he hated cats.

Tom went on to say he had tried to make friends with the man many times by jumping on his knee, but the man knocked him off each time. He told me sometimes he would claw and bite the man when he walked across the room, then run away. Then the man got very angry and threw a shoe at him.

Tom had excellent reasons for misbehaving, but I never encourage a cat to continue naughtiness because it can aggravate an already tense situation. Susan's husband was enraged and now insisted she put the cat down. Tom told me Susan was not happy with the man as he often shouted at her. Susan confirmed this, saying she stayed with her husband because of the children.

If you are an animal lover, it is important that your partner love animals, too. Otherwise you are bound to face problems, as Susan and Tom were.

Tom told me Susan put him outside at night when her husband came home but he meowed at the window and wakened everyone. He said Susan would let him in and put him in the kitchen, letting him out again in the morning before the man got up.

Susan said Tom's behavior was disturbing everyone's sleep. That morning things had come to a head when Susan's husband left his briefcase open on the kitchen floor while he went to answer the telephone, and Tom had sprayed all over the briefcase and papers inside. The man was so angry he had kicked Tom all the way to the door and then kicked him out into the garden. Susan began crying as she told me she'd spent two hours looking for Tom and had found him, shaking with fright and shock, hidden under the shed.

I told Susan she had to take steps to protect Tom from her husband. I gently pointed out she could never be happy with someone who was cruel and didn't love cats as she did. I knew Tom was not going to stop this behavior: He was trying to make a point. I also told Susan that cats don't forget an unkind action and Tom would never forgive her husband. I told her Tom needed a home filled with love and compassion, the kind he had experienced for the first five years of his life.

I suggested she find another home for Tom. In another home, Tom could be a perfect cat, just as he had been before her marriage. Two weeks later Susan called to say her mother would be taking Tom and could I explain to him why he was going there. She also asked me to tell him she would visit him. Susan was terribly upset about giving up Tom, but knew this was the best solution and the best choice and chance for her marriage.

As long as a cat feels special and is loved and appreciated, there should be no insurmountable problems. If trouble begins, assessing what has changed in the household in the last few months should help you unearth the cause of the trouble.

$\mathcal{R}$ambo

I am frequently a guest on radio and television shows, and each time the phone banks light up with calls from pet owners. I connect with animals through the owner's energy and talk to the animals live on the air.

Margaret called me one day very distressed about her cat, Rambo. She had just moved to another state and Rambo was no longer the happy contented cat he had been before the move. His personality had changed completely. He often bit her hand and Margaret was upset. She'd even considered moving back to Houston.

As I heard Rambo's silent language, the first feeling I received was anger and I acknowledged it. Telepathic language is very fast and I received a picture from him of the countryside. With my cat nose, I smelled grass and my feelings changed from anger to contentment in an instant. My whole cat form was receiving his language loud and clear. During the next few seconds, I felt my cat body being confined. It was like being in prison. Then I received a picture of the inside of a small house. I knew instinctively that Rambo had been used to being an indoor/outdoor cat and since the move, his human companion was no longer allowing him to go outdoors.

The next feeling I received from him was one of great sadness. It almost brought me to tears. I informed Margaret that Rambo wanted desperately to go outside into his natural world and the only way he knew to tell her was to bite her. Margaret told me he had been born as a farm cat.

I explained that all his life he had climbed trees, hunted, and played in the grass. When I explained to Margaret how Rambo felt, she told me she was afraid to let him outside because cats had been killed by coyotes in the area. That was why she had felt forced to make this drastic change. Her fear for her furry companion was justified, but she did not understand how difficult this change was for Rambo.

I explained that he must be allowed to go out and, with her help, I would explain the dangers to him. I also told her the biting would continue if she refused to allow him to explore his natural environment and that he could not understand why his loving human companion was treating him this way, since she had always allowed him absolute freedom before. Rambo also said that his cat door had not come with them on the move and asked why there was no door for him. He was very indignant about this.

Both Margaret and Rambo were very upset. If Margaret refused to allow him his freedom, Rambo would eventually become sick, because his quality of life was unbearable. If he had only experienced an indoor life, he would not have been suffering in the same way. Having his freedom taken away was devastating and confusing for him.

I told Margaret to visualize her garden as I talked to Rambo about the danger of the coyotes and what could happen to him if he left his territory. I used all my cat body to tell him of the dangers as I visualized a pack of coyotes tearing at my flesh and tossing my body about. I felt the fear and pain in my cat physical form and knew Rambo could feel it too. Now he could understand why his human companion was keeping him indoors.

I felt his fear as he received my telepathic communication. I explained he must stay in his garden where he would be safe. I once again told Margaret to visualize her garden. Then I told him to stay there and not to wander away. He agreed to this.

I told her whenever she thought of Rambo, to always see him in his garden. She was not to think, "I hope he has not ventured out again," because another picture would follow of him being outside the garden. He would receive the wrong picture and a worried emotion and could then do exactly what she feared.

Four weeks later, Margaret rang to say Rambo had not attempted to leave the garden. She told me his biting had diminished and they were enjoying a loving relationship once again. When I last talked to Rambo, he said he had a new friend called Miss Kitty. I received a feeling of happiness from him along with a picture of a small cat as he told me about her. Margaret confirmed she had rescued a cat from the shelter and that the two felines were getting along well.

Rambo further informed me he had told Miss Kitty about the dangers outside their territory. She always stayed with him in their garden, so he felt he'd taught her to be careful. I thanked him for telling me and informed Miss Kitty how lucky she was to have such a wise and loving companion. I then received a feeling of pride and joy from Rambo as he agreed with me.

Planning for Domestic Bliss and Harmony

When a happily engaged couple decides to get married, one party or both may wish to bring one or more pets. The normal adjustment process for newlyweds is often fraught with tension and the addition of pets, not necessarily of one species, can result in an explosion of emotion and misunderstanding. Sometimes misunderstandings about this can lead to lasting damage.

Here is a tragic example of how serious these misunderstandings can become, and how important it is to include in any premarital discussions how best to introduce and integrate all the domestic pets involved. Any discussion must include equal treatment of each animal as it is welcomed into the newly formed family.

A woman told me that she and her husband were distraught because her two cats would not stop meowing at night. The problem was perplexing as the cats, she informed me, had been perfectly behaved until the last six months. Her husband was particularly angry because he could not sleep due to their constant noise. During the day the cats were quiet.

When I connected to the cats, they immediately assured me they loved their human companion, Claire, but now they were living with a man who did not like cats. I realized that Claire had lived alone with her cats and I decided to get more information from them. I invited them to continue their story.

They told me that Claire loved them very much but when

they moved to their new house, this man, her new husband, who was now sharing Claire's bedroom, shut them out. Sadly, Claire confirmed this. I told Claire the cats missed sleeping with her. All she had to do to stop the meowing was to allow them back into her bedroom. The cats went on to tell me Claire's new husband did not feel the same way about them as Claire did. I explained to them that this alone was why they were not allowed to sleep with their mum in the bedroom.

After living with just Claire for five years, the cats were finding it hard to adjust to sharing her with a man. Also, they had moved house (which can be a traumatic experience for a cat), as well as being forced to give up sleeping at night with their beloved human companion. Their constant wailing and meowing was their way of telling her they were feeling neglected. The cats knew they were making Claire's new husband fractious as he was unable to sleep. I suggested that perhaps she could sleep with the cats in another room for a few hours every night. But the best solution would be for her husband to change his mind and learn to sleep with the cats. This would restore tranquility to the cats as well as to Claire and her husband.

I also suggested that her husband take a more active role in the cats' lives. Perhaps he could feed them and spend some time talking to them each day. I am sure Claire never thought a new, unsympathetic husband's views would affect her cats so dramatically. I hoped for an acceptable compromise and that she and her husband would be joined in the bedroom by her cats. But regretfully, I heard nothing further from Claire and my fear is that either the marriage foundered or the unhappiness of everyone in the house continues with little hope of any satisfactory resolution.

It may be a generalization, but the fact is that many intelligent, independent women choose to share their homes with cats while men tend to be more comfortable with dogs. Cats can be possessive and less than understanding if they feel they are being replaced in the affections of someone with whom they have shared their lives for years. Sensitivity and sympathy from both the owner and her new partner are essential if such problems are to be avoided.

Fighting

Few problems are more distressing for a cat lover than changes in feline behavior, especially if it leads to once passive mates fighting. Many of my clients consult me about this. Often they are so distraught, they are on the brink of giving up their animal for adoption. No cat lover wants to have to make that kind of decision.

Cats, like children, love attention and affection. When they feel they are being ignored they will seek it and don't much care if it is good or bad attention, as long as they get it. Yet cats are intelligent. They are well aware that if they misbehave, their human companions will notice.

A cat's body language can indicate if he is unhappy or distressed about something. When this results in an unacceptable behavioral problem, it is important to track backward and see when the first signs became obvious and then try to identify the source of the problem. Don't neglect to observe any messages contained within changes in your pet's mood and manner— people often make changes that will affect their cat without talking to the cat first. It's very important to tell the cat about changes in the household, particularly if the change is going to be permanent as in the case of a divorce or a death in the family. Even when the change isn't permanent, as when a child goes away to boarding school or college, it is important to explain things—the cat is part of the family, after all. Failing to include your cat may result in inappropriate behavior, as in the case of Duffy and Cinderella.

Duffy and Cinderella

A couple came to consult me about their two cats, Duffy and Cinderella, upset because over the past weeks the cats had begun fighting. These were fur-flying fights resulting in Duffy having to see the vet for a bite on his leg.

When I tuned in, I discovered they were two very angry cats. Formerly passive Cinderella told me she belonged to her mother and Duffy said he belonged to his dad. This gave me the first clue to the problem and the couple confirmed that each had owned their cat and lived alone with it before their marriage.

I picked up feelings of extreme worry from both of the cats. Duffy told me his dad was always shouting and quarreling with his wife. He loved his dad and didn't like him being upset.

An angry Cinderella said she didn't like this shouting either, especially when it was her mum being targeted. The relationship clearly wasn't happy and the human discord was causing the cat problem, with each cat taking his or her human's side, hence the fighting.

I explained to the amazed couple that the cats were upset because they were shouting at each other. I went on to tell them that the cats would have bonded if the couple had thought of them as part of a family, not as separate "his" and "hers" pets.

My clients confirmed their marriage was going through a difficult patch. They were both stunned at what their cats told me and asked me what they could do. I suggested that their relationship needed to change. They needed to start living as a family. Moreover, they should take turns feeding both cats together; the cats told me each had been fed separately by their own human. This was another reason why the cats took sides every time their humans had a disagreement.

I also suggested they tell the cats they were a family and that they all needed to take care of each other. It was up to the humans to put things right so the cats could feel integrated. This is another case where the people weren't having a cat problem . . . the cats were having a people problem!

Sunshine

Little Sunshine has been allowed to grow and explore her personality because her human companions understand cats and are happy to live with some "disruptive behavior" that is part of Sunshine's personality and is constantly entertaining and unpredictable.

My dear friend Diana, owner of an equestrian center, is a great animal lover who, in addition to owning and caring for her horses, takes in strays. Cats and dogs are constantly being dropped off at her horse barn.

One of the cats dropped off by uncaring people was a beautiful feline Diana named Emma. Emma was quite wild, so Diana fed her outside with a number of other cats that live in and around the stables and barns. A short time after Emma arrived, Diana noticed she was pregnant. Diana has had all the other cats neutered and spayed but Emma would have nothing to do with the humane cage Diana used for catching stray cats.

Over the next few weeks Emma was content living outside. Diana and her staff kept an eye on her. Diana has two dogs, a beautiful Rottweiler named Thor and a beagle called Sparky. Sparky loved Emma and followed her around. Emma reciprocated. The pregnancy went well but even when it was obvious Emma was in labor, she wouldn't allow anyone to catch her. The only one who could get close to her was Sparky.

Diana knew it was dangerous for Emma to have her kittens outside. A snake, King, lived under a tree over by the stables. Diana had developed a friendship with King and considered him part of the animal family. He was harmless to humans, but he might be a danger to small kittens.

The kittens were born but try as they might, no one was able to find them. After she finished eating, Emma consistently led

Diana in the wrong direction, taking her all over the property, but never to her kittens. Diana called me to talk to Emma and ask her where the kittens were. As I tuned in to Emma, I told her King could eat her kittens. She informed me she was constantly moving them and he would not find them.

I asked her again. She informed me she was not going to tell me where they were. I acknowledged her answer and told her that she and her kittens would be safer in Diana's house. She did not answer. I felt she was happy where they were.

After a few weeks a beautiful kitten walked out of a stand of bamboo. Diana grabbed it, and went to see if there were any more there. Sparky suddenly came up to Diana, gently holding a kitten in his mouth, looking very pleased with himself. As Diana reached down for the kitten, Emma came running. Diana picked up both kittens and ran into her house with Emma at her heels. Now both she and the kittens would be safe.

Emma adjusted very well to living inside with Diana and her husband and all their other cats, plus Sparky and Thor. The kittens were named Moonbeam and Sunshine. Sparky the beagle and Sunshine became inseparable, sleeping cuddled up together. Sparky would often pick her up in his mouth and put her in his bed. Emma did not seem to mind and was adjusting well to becoming a house cat. In fact, she welcomed Sparky's help.

Moonbeam and Sunshine had stolen Diana's heart, so no homes were going to be found for them. Sunshine began helping Diana with her bills. Each bill is chewed. Not a single one goes out to Diana's clients without Sunshine's tooth marks on the paper.

But Sunshine was developing more talents.

When Diana left the house, she invariably turned the television off. But when she came back the television was always on. Diana was perplexed, all the more so because Sunshine was always sitting in front of the TV watching it. Her small head would turn from side to side as she watched whatever was on the screen. Then one day Diana watched as Sunshine played with the remote control until the TV came on. The mystery was solved. Sunshine had learned to turn the TV set on by pushing buttons on the remote with her paws whenever she wanted entertainment.

Not long ago, Diana called me to tell me Sunshine's latest adventure. Diana had had a guest for dinner the evening before. Her guest had put her handbag on the floor. Back home, she called Diana, asking her to look around her house, as her checkbook and wallet were missing. She thought the contents might have spilled out without her noticing.

Diana knew Sunshine was clever and thought she might have been up to her tricks again. And of course, she always had the help of Sparky. There, behind the sofa, were the contents of Diana's guest's handbag. The checks had teeth imprints and the credit cards had also been chewed up a little. Fortunately, not too much damage was done and the contents of the handbag were returned to their rightful owner.

This beautiful cat, Sunshine, is turning out to be quite an extraordinary animal. She continues to raid every handbag that comes into the house. She has the ability to remove the contents one piece at a time. Then she hides her treasures.

Though this charming behavior is somewhat destructive at times, Sunshine makes up for it by making sure Moonbeam, Thor, and Sparky are never bored when she's around. After all, if their human companions are outside working, Sunshine can always turn on the TV for them all to watch!

Artist-in-Residence

Debbie shares her home with two thirteen-year-old felines: Ann, a beautiful white longhaired cat, and Alex, a part Persian.

As I tuned in to the cats, Ann told me to ask Debbie where her toy mice were. Debbie replied, "Ann chewed all the fur off of them," and said she was going to put them in the bin so Ann wouldn't eat them. Ann told me she was a very good chewer and chewed all of Debbie's clothing and the sheets. The astonished Debbie told me this was true as she pulled out the side of her jumper to show me a large round hole, beautifully and evenly chewed with a designer-frayed edging. Debbie found the "creative" side of Ann most annoying and did not appreciate her feline's artistic talent.

I explained to Debbie this chewing was a comfort to Ann and that she had been taken from her mother cat too young. Debbie confirmed this was so. Often, when a kitten has been taken from its mother too early, it begins to suck for comfort on something soft. In Ann's case, this resulted in many of Debbie's clothes and sheets having holes in them.

I asked Ann not to bite on clothes and sheets again. As I was talking to her, Ann sent me a picture of a peach-colored bathrobe and asked me if she could have it for her own. Debbie agreed when I explained she would still have the urge to chew. It would, at thirteen years old, be hard or impossible for her to stop, so the bathrobe would be hers to chew when she liked.

Ann informed me she loved the peach bathrobe and was very proud it was to be hers to chew. By giving Ann something with her scent on it, Debbie was making Ann very happy. Debbie called me two weeks later to say Ann did not chew on anything else.

Mr. Manchu, et al.

Melissa called to set up an appointment. She had four cats, and two of them were fighting. She had to get up during the night to intervene as the cats were pulling each other's hair out and their human companion was doing the same! Melissa's sleep was interrupted each night and she was frustrated. Giving up her cats was not an option because she loved them very much and just wanted them all to get along.

A few months previously, she had adopted two female cats, Snapdragon and Tater from a sanctuary. They were now companions to Mr. Manchu and Vernon, who had lived in harmony with their human companion for three years. As I tuned in to the cats, I could feel anger emanating from Mr. Manchu. Why had Melissa brought this horrible, smelly cat into their home? He was only angry with one of the cats, and Melissa confirmed this.

He was indignant toward Tater and hissed at her occasionally, but he was fighting with Snapdragon. Melissa thought both were to blame.

I find in cases like this, when new cats come into a home from a sanctuary and have, in the past, lived as outdoor cats, they often cause problems as they have already learned to fight for their domain. In this case, the scent of Mr. Manchu was upsetting the new arrivals. I could feel this by tuning in to Snapdragon again.

I then informed Snapdragon that I understood why she was fighting with Mr. Manchu and it was okay to fight for her domain outside, but she was inside now. I also informed her that I understood Mr. Manchu's scent reminded her of another cat from the past. I invited her to tell me about that cat.

As this was an emotional problem for Snapdragon, I had to find out the emotional reason before I could deal with the physical one, otherwise the fighting would not stop. Snapdragon then told me her story, which I have put into my own words:

The first human companions I lived with after being taken from my mother moved and left me behind. I was hungry and I waited each day by the window of the empty house, hoping they would come back, but they did not return.

I was so hungry. I had to find food.

When I was small, my mother had started to teach me to hunt for food but one day I was playing with my sister away from my mother and a human came and picked us up. She drove us in a car to her home. Then she gave me away to a family, but they did not take care of me. They fed me outside and one day moved away. After a few days of waiting for my family to return, I left home to search for food. I made friends with a tomcat who helped me. A lady was feeding many wild cats in her garden. My friend told me about her and showed me the way to her house.

There was a white cat there that would run me off, away from the food. My new friend would chase this cat away, so I could eat, but one day when I went for food, my old friend was not there, so the other cat went for me. I was very badly bitten. His scent was very similar to this cat in my new home.

I thanked Snapdragon again for telling me her sad story. I then explained to her that the fighting would have to stop, as this was upsetting for Melissa. I also informed Snapdragon that Mr. Manchu had allowed her to come into his home and I reminded her how kind that was of him. I could feel Mr. Manchu responding and agreeing with me.

I told Snapdragon again that I understood the scent of Mr. Manchu was much the same as the cat she had fought with, but that it was different, and she would have to get used to living with this scent. I told her she did not have to fight with Mr. Manchu. I then tuned in to Mr. Manchu, who informed me he stalked Snapdragon around the house. I asked him if he could stop doing this, and could he help Melissa take care of Snapdragon, as smart house cats don't stalk other cats. Then I went on to tell Mr. Manchu what helping to take care of the new cats involved.

I praised Mr. Manchu and told Melissa how important it was that she also praise him for helping her to care for the two new animals. I also thanked Tater. I did not want her left out, as she would have been upset.

A few weeks later, Melissa called to say the cats had stopped fighting for a few weeks after I talked to them, but now the problem was back. I once again tuned in to both Mr. Manchu and Snapdragon. I thanked them for not fighting for a while and asked them again to stop the fighting, praising them both and telling them again that smart cats don't fight. A few weeks passed by and I called Melissa to see how the cats were. She informed me that all the cats were now getting along well with each other.

In some cases, I find I do have to follow up and remind the cats they don't have to continue with this behavior. By talking to them and acknowledging how this can upset their human companions, I find most cats are quite reasonable about changing their behavior. But usually I find that if the human is prepared to offer love and understanding and treat the cats with kindness, their pets are willing to comply with their human companion's wishes. Melissa put all of this into practice and the cats wanted to please her.

In this chapter we have discussed some of the ways a feline can misbehave if it is unhappy or feeling neglected. Among the most painful and difficult times a cat lover has to face is when a cat goes missing. Read on to discover some of the many reasons why a feline may decide to leave home.

Chapter Six

When Cats Leave Home

CATS "leaving home"? The idea of this might appear to stretch the bounds of credibility for a few people. Can it really be that many domestic cats make a conscious decision to leave the apparent peace and tranquility of their home for the risks and uncertainties of an outdoor existence? If the predominant impression of our friendly felines is one of purring contentment stretched out by the hearthside or wrapping themselves sinuously around our ankles, then such action might well be classified as feline insanity.

However, one of the eternally fascinating and sometimes frustrating aspects of the relationship between the feline and his human companion is the eventual realization that despite all the outward manifestations of affection the feline has an inner steel of character, and can on occasions, for what might appear baffling reasons, display an independence that sometimes calls into question whether the relationship is really a meeting of equals based on love and understanding. Exactly who is calling the tune?

I am consulted frequently by distraught owners whose cats are missing and, while there may be a wide variety of straightforward explanations, there are all too many times when the owner is responsible for the feline departure.

These runaway cats are normally angry. They know their human companion will be upset but they have taken this extreme measure because they have concluded that they do not wish to tolerate the domestic environmental or atmospheric conditions prevailing in their present home and decide to leave.

When I connect telepathically with a lost cat, I acknowledge everything he tells me. The astonished owners, while confirming that the information I have received is accurate, are often dismayed at the dissatisfaction and complaints registered from someone with whom they thought they were enjoying a rewarding relationship.

Generally speaking, the warning signs of unhappiness, and the potential for escalation into a major problem, are clear. If we are sensitive enough to recognize and interpret them we can take remedial action. As I've already said, we owe it to our pet to be alert to any behavioral changes and these are often caused by some distraction or worry of our own, be it romantic, professional, domestic, or a health preoccupation.

If the feline has left home because he is angry with his human companion, he may not be keen to be reunited with his owner unless the owner is prepared to deal with the underlying problems and begin to treat him with respect and understanding. I talk to the cat to find out what caused him to leave, then relay this back to the owner. My object is to get to the root of the problem and see if I can find a way to reunite them. If I can, with the owner's cooperation, convince the cat that the areas of concern that caused him to leave will be dealt with I can then concentrate on analyzing the information I am receiving from him and narrow down the area where he might be, in order to mount a targeted search.

Some cats remember their journeys clearly while others will be confused. Often they will send me a picture of a distinctive landmark that can help the owner in his search. I tell a frightened or confused cat to wait until it is late at night, as cats normally feel safer when things are quieter. I tune in to the cat's energy, reassuring him and telling him to trust his instincts, that I am with him and he is not alone on his journey. I encourage him and tell him that he is very clever, and confirm the route he should follow to find his way home. I tune in to my "cat ears" to check for noise before telling a cat to cross a street. I feel the hard surfaces with my paws and smell car and truck fumes with my nose. If there is noise (maybe a car approaching) I tell the cat it must be still and wait before crossing. I send the message with my mind but also with my body so the cat understands what he must do to travel safely.

If a cat has helped and we have targeted an area, I sometimes have the human use drops of his own urine to mark a trail home. The cat's sense of smell is acutely strong and he can pick up his human's scent from quite a distance. The scent is particularly important as it can also have a calming effect, reassuring and comforting the cat so it can better use its basic instincts to help find the correct direction homeward. However, occasionally the cat will find the return journey too daunting and he will stay in his new territory making a new home there.

Now I would like to share a few case histories of cats who decided to leave home but who relented and were persuaded to return to their now enlightened owners.

$\mathcal{K}$ato

One day Fitz received a call from Barbara, who lives in California. Her beloved cat Kato was missing. Fitz booked the appointment quickly since lost animals are my priority.

When Barbara called, I connected to Kato immediately. He was indignant and very annoyed with her. I told Barbara he could hear her calling for him and he knew her husband was out searching for him with a torch at night, so he had to be hiding quite close to the house. I asked him why he left. His list of complaints came fast and furious. I acknowledged them and relayed them to Barbara.

1. The new dog, Sabrina, was playful and noisy. She pushed his ball around and ate from his dish.

2. Kato felt the dogs had received more presents at Christmas than he. He sent me a picture of red collars on the dogs' necks. Both of the dogs had been given special Christmas collars. He wanted a new collar too, but Mummy hadn't given him one.

3. Barbara had let her hair grow long and he didn't like it. The Barbara he loved and had grown up with had short hair. Now she had long hair just like all the dogs, and as her husband had long hair with a pony tail, this left him as the only one in the household with short hair.

4. Mummy was not giving him his special drink anymore. When I told Barbara this, she said she usually bought special milk formulated for cats but during the Christmas rush had not had time to get it.

5. Kato was unhappy that strange men had come into his room and taken his bed. Barbara explained she had a guest staying for Christmas and had bought a new bed for the guest bedroom. Kato informed me the smell of the new bed was unfamiliar and he wanted the old bed back.

6. Barbara had stopped giving Kato his treats a few weeks back because they tended to cause flare-ups in his FUS (Feline Urologic Syndrome). But he missed them.

I told Barbara that Kato didn't understand why she'd stopped giving him treats. He informed me he was also still upset about a dinner party some weeks before, as one of the guests didn't like cats. He asked me why Barbara had invited someone that did not like him. He thought it very insensitive of her to invite people that didn't like cats. Besides, Kato didn't like the noise the visitors made. How dare they come into *his* house when he was used to a tranquil atmosphere?

The astonished Barbara confirmed that this was all true. Once Barbara knew why Kato had decided to leave, she told him she was very sorry and promised she would make everything right by getting back all the things he loved. I told Barbara she should consider buying his treats and special milk, as he would not return until all his demands had been met and he would know since he was on a direct line of communication with her.

I then suggested to him that he could return home when it grew dark. I informed him that Barbara was very upset and had not realized she had been the cause of him leaving home. I told him she loved him very much and she would make sure none of these things happened again. He told me he would think about it.

That was big of him, wasn't it? But typical. I believe that in general cats are confident of their own ingenuity and feelings of superiority in their dealings with their human companions and can be duplicitous in achieving their goals. They can affect studied indifference, feigned disdain, petulance, real intransigence, and display overwhelming affection—all orchestrated with consummate guile. Who is in charge here? Perhaps they are indeed benevolent despots or subtle dictators—expert in achieving domination without their subjects being aware of it.

Anyway, back to Kato. That night, just as darkness was falling, he arrived on the doorstep. Barbara was so happy to see him she cried with joy. He now receives lots of attention and affection. And when Barbara purchases gifts, she remembers all the animals. Barbara also tells Kato before visitors come and makes sure he is in her bedroom with the door closed when visitors arrive.

Bugsy

Sara's beloved cat Bugsy was missing.

When I connected to Bugsy, he was very sad and upset. He began by telling me a man had taken him, put him in his van, and driven him a long way from home. Bugsy sent me pictures of piles of old car tires and an old barn. He also remembered some of the journey so I was able to describe it to Sara.

She knew the area Bugsy described and she guessed who had taken him. A deliveryman, with whom she had been angry, had been back to her house when she was out and had left a parcel on her doorstep. Bugsy had been outdoors and Sara informed me that she feared he had been catnapped.

I told Sara about the area where Bugsy had been put out of the van. I suggested she go there and get down on her hands and knees so she could see the world as Bugsy described it, reminding her that the world looks very different from human height. I also told her to collect as much of her urine as possible in a container, and to leave droplets of it near the barn. Cats have a very strong sense of smell and Bugsy would feel happy to know she had been there. By placing her scent at the barn and at places along the road home, it would encourage Bugsy to find his way home and provide recognizable landmarks.

Bugsy continued to send me pictures. There were many other cats there with him. He sent me pictures of some of them.

Sara told me she went to the barn where the old tires were stacked but didn't see Bugsy, only a few wild cats, and when she called, Bugsy did not come out. I explained to Sara that when cats are frightened, they might not respond even when their trusted owner calls them.

Each morning I continued to connect with Bugsy, urging him to find his way home. As he started his journey he was able to pick up Sara's scent. I encouraged him to follow it by telling him he was a smart cat and I was with him. I explained that he must stay away from the road. I was able to tell him this by being a cat myself, and feeling my paws on the hard surface of the road as well as smelling oil and petrol fumes. Then I changed the picture and imagined the look and smell of grass and the soft feeling under my feet. Grass would be safer to travel on when that was possible. Bugsy asked me if I were a cat. I told him yes, but I was also a human.

Bugsy knew Sara had been to where he was living because he had picked up her scent. He wanted to be reunited with his family. Using his heightened senses he could instinctively tune in to the universal energy fields and could feel the pull of the family's energy like a built-in compass. When he tuned in to Sara's energy, he became confident about making his way home.

Bugsy was using all his senses as he traveled homeward. He was listening for cars on the road as well as watching for them. I told him to continue following his instincts and he would find his way back. Within a week I had a joyous call from Sara. Bugsy was home where he belonged.

Points of View Differ

Many cats dislike being taken out of their environment. If at all possible, arrange for your cat to be cared for at home when you travel. The smell of strange places can be distressing and disturbing to most felines.

Since a cat's point of view isn't often heard or taken into account, many cat owners don't understand that a cat will leave home if he feels neglected or has had to endure too many changes. Pele's story illustrates how even the most caring owners don't always get things right from the cat's angle.

Pele

Sidgwick & Jackson are my publishers in the United Kingdom. Naomi worked very hard on the book promotion tour of *What the Animals Tell Me* and accompanied me on TV and radio shows. She called one morning to ask if I could help get her sister's missing cat back. Pele had been missing for over two weeks and Naomi's mother and sister were very distressed.

When I connected to Pele, she was angry that her humans had gone away and left her. Not only that, but they had also taken her to this horrible, smelly place called the cattery. She had always stayed at home before with a nice lady who came in to feed and talk to her. Pele loved this arrangement. The smell of her home was familiar and reassuring.

Cats recognize things by smell and love to have familiar smells around them. Going to board at the cattery was like going to prison for her. All the smells and noises were unfamiliar and there were dogs barking all day long. What's more, she was shut in a cage and had other cats hissing at her. How could her human companions do this to her?

When the family had gone on holiday in previous years, a lady who lived nearby had taken care of Pele at home. Unfortunately, the neighbors were going away at the same time this year and were unable to care for her, so Naomi's family had taken Pele to the cattery where she would be safe and well looked after. To her human companions, this had been the best solution but to Pele it was unacceptable.

I explained to Pele why this had occurred and how sorry her human companions were to have upset her. Pele went on to tell me she had also had a disgusting change of food. She had been put on a light diet. She wanted her proper food back.

I explained she could change her mind about running away and come back home. I promised her humans would get all her favorite things again. She confided that tuna was her favorite food and she would like to eat it regularly if she was to come home. She also missed her dishes. I confirmed to her how much her human family loved her. They were prepared to meet all her requests and make sure she had a luxurious lifestyle if she decided to return.

She weakened and said she missed her human's bed, how comfortable it was and how she loved all the cushions but wondered what had happened to her toy. It was no longer on the bed before she left and she wanted it back. She continued to tell me how worried she was about her "mother," who had a problem with her leg and couldn't make it work properly. I explained to Pele that her human "mother," who had had polio as a child, was not in pain even though her leg was damaged. Her "mother" missed her and needed Pele to take care of her. I told Pele how upset the family was at her disappearance and repeated how much they all loved her. I sent pictures of her coming home as darkness fell.

I explained to Pele's owners not to ever leave her at the cattery again. If they did, Pele would leave home for good. I felt Pele was very close to home. I again reminded her she could change her mind about leaving and come home before darkness.

And that's just what she did.

The following day I received a beautiful bouquet of flowers at my hotel room from Naomi. The flowers were lovely but the joy they give me could not compare to the joy I feel every time another furry companion comes back home.

$\mathcal{L}$ucky

My client Cathy lives with her husband, Jerry, and fourteen poodles as well as a variety of other animals, both wild and domestic. Three of the wild animals are cats that live in her garden in Houston.

Cathy's other home is in Arizona. She and Jerry travel between the two. One day Cathy was sitting in her garden in Arizona when a small straggly cat jumped up on the brick wall. The cat was quite unconcerned about the two dogs running around the garden and barking. After a while the cat left. That night, Cathy put additional food out because she was concerned about his scrawny form, and hoped he would show up. At about 10 P.M., the cat appeared outside the window, jumped on the table, and demolished the food.

A week later, Cathy was back to Houston. She had booked an appointment with me for Wednesday morning to talk to her animals and her new cat friend in Arizona, whom she had named Lucky. As I tuned in to him I found him to be quite chatty and very pleased that Cathy was feeding him. Cathy wanted me to explain that she did not live at the house all the time. Before she left Arizona, she had bought a cat feeder and water dispenser so he would have dry food and water while she was away. A friend who liked cats was going to make sure the food dispenser and water dispenser were kept filled.

Cathy also wanted me to convey to him that he could stay inside the garden and sleep under the porch where she had placed a dog kennel for him to use if the weather was cold or wet. He quickly informed me he was already using the doghouse and to thank her. He told me he loved to live outside and that this was the only place he had ever lived.

Over the next few months, Cathy continued to travel between Houston and Arizona and Lucky would visit each night for the wet food she put out while she lived at the house. When she went to Houston, he would eat the dry food. In the evening of the day Cathy arrived at the house in Arizona, Lucky's face would appear at the window, then he would jump up on the garden table and eat and stay for a while. Occasionally she would see him in the yard during the day.

When she visited Arizona in July, Cathy was very upset when Lucky didn't make his usual appearance. She put out food and called his name, but no Lucky. After a week, Cathy was very alarmed. Cathy had booked another telephone appointment and as I tuned in to Lucky, I could feel his sadness. At the same time, there was tremendous pain under my fingernails. I knew Lucky was alive but someone had had him declawed. I asked him to tell me what had happened and where he was. I could feel his confusion and fear. He began by telling me he was a house cat now. He had gone into a garden where he had been many times, where a lady put out food. She had been putting the food in a crate, and Lucky often went there but since he could get out, he wasn't concerned. The last time he went into the crate to eat, there was a *bang*, and he was trapped.

He was put into a car and driven to a place where there were many dogs and cats in cages. He was placed in another cage where he stayed until a human came and looked at his teeth and felt him all over. Then he could not remember any more until he woke up. Now he was living in a house. The humans were very kind to him, but his paws hurt so much. Then he began to cry. He wished he could see Cathy again and go to her house.

I explained everything to Cathy. She was extremely upset that he had been declawed. Over the next six months, whenever Cathy had a consultation, I would talk to Lucky. He would tell me how much he missed the scent of the outdoor life and that, if he could get out of the house, he would run away. He said how he missed the smell of the green grass and the earth as he remembered lying on the soil, his body stretched out, as the sun warmed him. He remembered how he sharpened his claws on trees and stretched his back and muscles.

One evening, as Fitz and I sat in the garden with all our animals around us, I felt Lucky on my telepathic line, telling me he had escaped from the house and was happy to be free again. I gave Cathy the good news. She was overjoyed and was ready to catch the next plane to Arizona. I explained that Lucky was going to be very nervous for a while, and he might not let her see him. It would take him time to learn to trust humans again.

Two weeks later, Cathy arrived in Arizona, hoping to see Lucky. Each night she put out food for him, but Lucky would not visit until she had gone to bed. In the morning the dish would be empty. This went on for two months. Lucky would talk to me each week. I asked him if he would show himself to Cathy because she was very upset that he would not come back into the garden and let her see him. The following day, Cathy was sitting by the pool, when she saw something moving in the bushes. There was Lucky. He walked across the patio and disappeared into more bushes. Cathy was overjoyed.

It has taken Lucky four months to return to visiting on a regular basis, but now he is back, jumping on the table for food each night, and is gradually gaining confidence and beginning to trust humans again. Cathy knows he will have to rely on humans for food, as it is more difficult for him to hunt since his claws have been removed. Sadly, he can no longer climb trees nor is he able to defend himself should another animal attack him.

Declawing is a frightful practice, usually done to protect people's furniture and curtains. There is no doubt that damage can occur when cats sharpen their claws on furniture and fabric. If a cat's claws are too long they can snag furniture and mark wood. A cat claws like this to mark its territory. When a cat is not confined to the house, it will claw trees and fences. The claw marks leave a ragged design as a visual sign to other cats. A ragged design on a tree or fence or the fabric of your furniture conveys the cat's position within its territory in a manner similar to spraying.

Scratching and stretching on a scratching post is preferable to your cat's scratching the furniture. With patience, you can train your cat to use a post. Rubbing catnip on the post can sometimes attract older cats to scratching posts. And there are new cardboard scratching boxes, also containing catnip, which can be enticing to cats of all ages, but it's far easier to train them as kittens by playing with them and getting them into the habit of stretching and scratching where you want them to.

If your cat scratches wooden furniture, try spreading aluminum foil over your chair legs and put the scratching post close to the table or legs your cat is scratching. Tabasco sauce rubbed on wooden furniture also acts as a good deterrent. Show your cat where the post is, and gently transfer his scratching to the post. Always get rid of the scratch marks he has made. Refinish the wooden surface or, if the material is frayed, get rid of the visible frays.

It is essential, particularly for indoor cats, that you provide something, preferably something rough, for them to scratch on. All cats need to scratch. Some cats love scratching on rough doormats, or a log or carpet scraps. Whatever you choose, make sure it's always available to your cat.

Cyril

Occasionally, there's a cat that leaves home and just won't come back. Cyril was one of these.

Anita, his human friend, was quite upset at the absence of her cat Cyril but when she arrived home one day, Anita did not yet realize Cyril had actually left for good. When I connected to Cyril, he told me he no longer wanted to live with Anita and ten other furry friends. He was fed up with having to share all his dishes with two dogs that constantly ate his food and with several cats he didn't even like.

One of the stray cats living outside had given birth under the garden shed. The last straw came when all the kittens were moved into the house, because Anita had not asked him if they could come into his home. Cyril was very upset and told me he had been marking his territory inside his home by spraying the space he wanted for himself, thereby telling the other cats to stay away. But no matter how much he sprayed his territory, the other cats came into his space.

He even decided to put his scent on the bed, but the other cats still came on to the bed he shared with his human mother. This angered him. By putting his scent on the bed he was telling the other cats this was his place and the other cats shouldn't sleep on it. He said his human mother was angry about a cat spraying on the bed, but she didn't know which one had done it.

As I tuned in to Cyril, I could feel his full stomach. I asked him where he was. He told me the route he had traveled leaving home and sent me pictures of apartments and steps about half a mile away. Anita recognized the descriptions I gave her.

He also said he had found a very nice new home with a single lady. He had lived as an only cat before and liked being on his own with his new human friend. He had new dishes and plenty of food that was only for him. He liked his new home very much and had no intention of returning. He was happy.

I told Anita how he felt. She was upset and left in tears.

A day later, armed with posters of Cyril, Anita drove to the apartments and displayed her posters. In response, a lady named Gale telephoned to tell Anita she had found a cat like Cyril and he was living with her. I explained to Anita that if she took Cyril back, he would definitely leave again because he was unhappy living with other cats. He still loved her, but things had changed drastically for him since he first came to live with her.

When he first came, he was the only cat and he had all of Anita's attention. He liked life that way.

After Anita increased her cat family, he was unhappy living with so many others and decided to find another home. At his new home, his dishes were his, his bed was his, and what's more, all the toys his new human companion had bought for him were his and his alone.

All cats are different, just like humans. Occasionally, I find a cat that wants to live alone with a human companion and does not need to be with other cats. Cyril was one of those. He was happy being an only cat. Once Anita knew Cyril was happy, she went over to meet Gale. After this Anita decided to leave Cyril with her. Gale had just lost her pet to cancer and it was obvious she loved Cyril. Anita visits Gale and Cyril regularly and is happy knowing he has a good home. Cyril is always happy to see Anita and always shows her great affection.

There are times like this when returning home is not the best thing for the feline. They need to be in an environment that makes them happy. In this case, Cyril is the answer to Gale's prayer for companionship and Gale is the answer to Cyril's wish to be the only pet in the family. But there was another cat that wouldn't come home for very different reasons.

Alex

Sarah and Tom arrived at my office for their appointment. They had both been to see me previously about their cat companions.

On the set of my new show, *The Pet Psychic*, which throws up
all sorts of animal problems. © DCI/Discovery Virtual Library

At the age of fourteen
with one of my first cats.

With Fitz and some of our animals

When we rescued Rosie
from a trailer park, she was
unable to feed herself, she
was pregnant, undernourished
and living in fear.

When the vet had almost
given up hope, Linda asked
me to try and heal Willie.
Together we saved Willie
from dying of poisoning.

When Sophie first moved in she was constantly hiding under the sofa. Though it took her a little while to adjust, Patrick was determined to help her enjoy her life like the special cat she is.

When Emma got married, Cinnamon and Raisin had to live with another cat, Honey. Honey helped the pair adjust to living as indoor/outdoor cats, staying close when they ventured outside.

When Emma's friend Manny was diagnosed with a serious illness,
Rex chose to return with his owner to Manny's childhood home
where they could spend time together.

With Sparky's help, Sunshine has learnt to raid any handbag
she can get her paws on. Then she hides her treasures all over the house.
She also likes to turn on the TV to entertain her furry friends!

Lucky was a victim of de-clawing and was forced to live
as an indoor cat. Since he ran away, Cathy has been feeding
him and slowly restoring his trust in humans.

When his human companions divorced, Jasper was devastated and
howled every night because he missed his human dad's scent.

Carol had no way of knowing that her new boyfriend's children had been chasing Princess, invading even her safest hiding places.

Marcia's dog Margaux immediately recognised Leonardo's spirit when he returned to the earth plane in the form of Hennessey.

After 21 years with Wellington, I sensed that he had returned
to me once again as Rosie's little kitten Dante.

This time their beloved cat Alex was lost. They had put up posters and contacted Animal Control but had had no response. Losing a cat is always devastating and Alex had been missing for over a week and they thought he must be dead.

Before they even sat down I reassured them that Alex was alive and that I was already communicating with him.

Alex was extremely angry. Complaints flowed fast and furious. Why had Sarah taken his ball away and changed his bowl and his food? The food no longer tasted like it used to. Why did his other cat companions have nicer food? He also complained the dog was extremely greedy and sometimes ate his food.

Sarah said she'd broken his dish and was very sorry. She also explained he was putting on weight so she had decided to give him a light diet. But Alex's complaints continued. The new human baby was now walking like a cat, Alex said, not like a proper human. I smiled as I realized he meant the baby was crawling. And sometimes the baby pulled his fur, hurting him. On top of that, Alex said his dishes were constantly being moved and he didn't know where to find his food.

Sarah told me the baby was crawling and did sometimes get into the cat food, so they had decided to take the cats' dishes up off the floor. Moving the dishes out of the baby's reach was a logical move for a human, but not for Alex. He liked his dishes where they had always been.

Alex said he felt very sad at home, so he had decided to leave. He said his other cat companions didn't like the disruption from the baby either, but they put up with it since they felt they had no choice. The human baby always came first. Most cats get upset about a change in routine but not many go to the extreme of leaving home, as Alex did.

Alex further informed me that his mummy had thrown him off the bed and made him sleep outside. Sarah's eyes filled with tears. She said she had to be sure the baby was safe. It was not easy taking care of a new baby and all the animals, too.

Alex continued, saying his mummy shouted constantly and threw him outside and called him names. Sarah confirmed she had called him a "dumb cat" as she put him outside in the yard.

Tom was quite sad when he heard how Alex felt and both of them began to understand why he had decided to leave. Until the baby came, the animals had been happy with their human companions. They were Sarah and Tom's children and their lifestyle was peaceful and tranquil. But the new addition to the family had disrupted the whole household. This can be a traumatic time for a new mother and extremely trying for a couple. Add to that several animals to consider and things become even more difficult.

Alex went on to say his dad would sometimes leave home angry and Sarah was always shouting at him. When they heard this they laughed. I reminded them never to underestimate how much their cats understand. Alex now told me he had a new life and still lived very close to his old house. He'd made a new feline friend, a beautiful ginger cat who didn't have a long tail like him. Sarah's eyes grew wide and she exclaimed, "I've seen that cat outside. He's a stray. I can't believe it. How did you know?"

That kind of reaction always amuses me as they had booked

an appointment so I could talk with their cat. Yet clients are often astonished at how much accurate information I receive.

Alex told me he was happy. A kind lady who loves cats was feeding him in the garden. He and his new friend liked to hunt together. He enjoyed the taste of fresh meat much more than the food Sarah had been giving him, so he was not going to go back.

I told Sarah and Tom he was living to the left of their home and the lady who fed stray cats was less than a quarter of a mile away. Alex told me again, he was not going back to live at the house with the horrible human baby. I had to explain to Tom and Sarah that if a cat decides it is not returning home, as Alex had, nothing will make him change his mind. Both Tom and Sarah were very upset when they left my office, but they respected the decision Alex had made and understood why he had decided to make the change in his life.

Introducing a New Baby or Pet into a Household

Pet owners can often run into unexpected trouble when a new baby or pet is brought into the home. It is important that any cats already living in the home do not feel displaced. A baby's arrival is a huge adjustment for the parents but it is also an adjustment for pets. It can be quite difficult to achieve a balance between the new baby's demands and your animals'.

I stress to my clients the importance of communicating the news of the new arrival to your cat before you bring the baby home. Include your cat in the decision-making process by discussing his new role with him ahead of time. Tell him you will need his help in caring for the new arrival and you could not manage without him. Emphasize how much you love him and what an important role he plays in your family. It's a good idea to play tapes of babies crying and gurgling so your cat or other animals can get used to the sounds.

Once the baby is at home with you, when you bring the baby into the room to feed, give your cat a special treat and talk to him, so he associates the baby with treats, good times, and attention. If you exclude him when the baby is with you, he will associate the baby with unhappiness and neglect.

If you fail to spend time with your cat at this time your cat is likely to blame the newcomer for the neglect and any other problems that arise. In some instances this can result in your cat showing his disapproval by various behavioral changes or by even deciding to leave home, as was the case with Alex.

Alex never came home, but many times the results are happier, as in the case of Peter and Ronda's cat, Taiway.

Taiway

Taiway had been missing for three months when Peter and Ronda Edwards called me from Montreal. They had contacted two other animal communicators, both of whom had told them their cat, a beautiful grey longhair, had been stolen. Both said he was living in a house with a family. After seeing me on TV, Peter set up an appointment with me.

I informed Peter and Ronda that I would do my best to get Taiway back but warned that some cats refuse to come home unless their human family is serious about making the changes they request. I added that most missing cats decided to leave home and usually have good "cat" reasons why they should do so. Within seconds I was communicating with Taiway. I could feel nervousness and instinctively knew this was not a cat that would allow a stranger to pick her up and take her away. She was the kind of cat who would use claws and teeth to defend herself. She was agile enough to evade a human trying to catch her. Peter confirmed this.

I began to receive Taiway's anger and stubbornness. She told me her family had moved and a new baby had come and caused havoc. The baby upset her food dishes and was constantly grabbing her fur and pulling on her tail. Ronda told me to assure Taiway they would not allow this to happen again if she came home. Taiway could hear Ronda and said she would think about it. I was pleased, as this was a good response.

Taiway also told me a huge dog lived close by the new house and frightened her when she went outside. She didn't like the way it barked at her. Everything in her life had changed drastically: there had been a change of house; her human companions used to talk to her all the time and now they were always talking to the baby; and now her dad went away from the house all day. Peter explained that was correct: He had worked from home before the move.

Indoors there was a new baby and outside there was a frightening dog. There was nothing she could rely on, not even her human companions, so she decided to leave and rely on herself. Cats are extremely independent. Taiway saw little benefit in co-operating with her human family as she felt they were not caring for her as they used to.

I listened to her side of the story and acknowledged everything she told me. Both human companions understood her point of view and told her they were very sorry. I explained she could change her mind about coming home. Winter was coming. It would be cold outside. I asked if she would tell me where she was and which way she had left the house. She sent me a picture of some rusty old cars where she was now living and a picture of other cats around her. Then she started telling me with her body, by transmitting to my body, of her journey. I felt my body going to the left and then to the right. Something soft was under my paws and I smelled grass. Then I could feel fear and smell petrol fumes. She was now near the road. I felt it was about a mile from home. Then again there were pictures of old cars, broken concrete, and a large warehouse.

Peter told me he knew where this building was but when he went there to look for Taiway, he saw other cats and realized a cat could hide under the broken concrete. I told him Taiway was there and had seen him searching with a torch at night but she would not come out. Taiway remained indignant as she told me she now had her own cat friends and her own life and she was not going back to her human family. She had found the human family changes very upsetting. Now she could rely on herself and her cat friends. She was still very angry.

There was a lady who fed them on a silver-colored metallic plate. Peter confirmed he had spoken to this lady and he had seen the large metal platter she fed them from. I reminded Taiway of the love Peter and Ronda had for her for many years and how much they missed her. That's why they had contacted me to ask her to please come home to them. They promised they would do anything to have her back.

She asked me if I were a cat. I told her when I spoke to cats, I became one, but I was a human who had a special gift that allowed me to talk to cats as well as humans. I said I lived in the cat world as well as in the human world. Taiway found this intriguing. I told her that I knew she could find her way home and I would help her. I said it was very hard on her human companions for her to stay away so long. I reassured her the dog outside would not hurt her and said she would have a steady routine again.

Taiway told me she loved Peter and Ronda and yes, she could always feel their love. They also constantly told her she was beautiful. But then the baby came and was very spoiled. She needed to be spoiled, too. Again I suggested Taiway go home. Ronda needed her to help look after the baby. The baby belonged to her as well as to Ronda and Peter. They were all a family.

I felt her pride and reminded her if she returned home she would be spoiled along with the baby. She told me she would like to have tuna fish often. I told her she could have tuna as soon as she returned home. It would be her first meal. She said she was having only dry food where she was. Ronda promised to put out sardines that night. This fish, like tuna, is regarded as a treat by most cats.

I reminded her again that the weather was going to be very cold. I said I would be with her if she decided to make the journey back to Peter and Ronda. I told her smart cats could easily find their way home in the dark and I tuned in with my "cat" ears so she received the idea to use her ears to listen for cars before crossing the street. I could feel she was thinking about going home. I again urged her to travel at night. She told me she would think about it.

After the consultation, I told Peter and Ronda to make all the changes Taiway had requested and to talk to her and tell her how sorry they were. She would know if they had made the changes and would hear them talking to her. Two days later, Taiway arrived home, three months after she'd left. Peter and Ronda were overjoyed.

Most people don't realize that, when I have a consultation about a lost cat, my work does not end when I hang up the telephone. Each night I connect with the cat's energy, urging him or her to come home, telling him or her I am with them. Many cats make the journey at night and arrive the next day. Cats sometimes stay watching their house until they're ready to approach. They may hide under a bush and be nervous about coming inside, but eventually, in their own time, they will appear.

When Fitz receives a phone message and comes to say, "Congratulations! You brought another cat home," it always brings us as much joy as it does to its human companions.

Chapter Seven

Litter Box Problems

PERHAPS nothing makes pet owners angrier than when their cat has problems with becoming house-trained or using the litter box. Ruined furniture, carpets and clothing, the constant cleaning, and the unpleasant smell all combine to make this one of the main reasons why people seek my help.

According to the American Veterinary Association, this type of problem is the top reason pets are given up for adoption and also the number one explanation given by families asking a vet to euthanize an animal that is not ill. As with all pet problems, there are always logical reasons for accidents. A change in routine or something as simple as a litter box being moved, or the color being changed can upset the cat and bring on a problem. Cats are sensitive about their litter boxes and hate change. Something we consider trivial can upset a feline.

Clean Creatures

Cats are creatures of habit and very clean animals. If you neglect keeping their litter box fresh and scooped out, the cat will find another place to go, simple as that. In a multi-cat household, some cats will share a litter box but others won't.

Training

Most mother cats "potty train" their young. Indoor cats will train their kittens to use a litter box. Occasionally, in a multi-cat household where the mother will allow it, another member of the cat "family" will step in to train the kittens. I've heard of cases where the "grandmother" cat helped out by taking over the litter box training of her daughter's kittens.

But if the kitten is taken away from the mother too early, it's up to you. If the kitten is quite young, you may need to stimulate it to defecate and urinate. The mother cat does this by licking its genitalia. *You* can use a piece of cotton wool dipped in lukewarm water. Always place the kitten in a litter box when doing this, to give it the sense of where to go.

Older kittens simply need to be taken to the litter box often. If an "accident" has occurred, place some of that urine or feces in the litter box to give the cat a scent signal. Once a proper litter box pattern has been established, keep the litter box clean.

Location Is Everything

Cats, like humans, have diverse personalities. Humans often think, "This is what I want my cat to do, so he must do it," without considering the cat's preferences. Yet something like litter box location is extremely important to a cat. You may decide to move it but your cat is used to the location, so she continues to defecate in her accustomed place, even though the litter tray is no longer there.

I receive many calls about cat "accidents." My first question is always, "Have you moved the litter box?" If the answer is yes, I tell them to move the box back to its original place and the problem is solved. Some cats don't mind a change of location but are upset by a new color or smell or a change in the type of litter.

If you decide to change your cat's litter box, leave the old box by the new one, no matter how inconvenient it may seem, until the cat begins using the new box. Then it's usually okay to remove the old box. When introducing a new type of litter, it's best to do it gradually, adding some to the old-style stuff and gradually increasing the amount of new litter until the change has been accomplished.

What's Happening?

Cats can become very worried when they sense their human companions are upset. One of the first ways this unhappiness manifests itself is with soiling accidents. This is the cat's way of telling you, "I am unhappy with what is happening here."

Such difficulties are never the cat's fault and can always be traced back to an emotional problem or a change in the family's routine.

Questions to ask yourself:

Have you moved the litter box or bought a new one?

Has there been a change in food?

Have you bought a new food bowl and removed the old one?

Is there a new arrival or human baby in the house?

Has a family member been ill or away?

Has there been a death in the family?

Has there been unusual stress or discord in your home?

Have you been giving your cat special attention every day?

Once you determine what factors have changed in the weeks preceding your cat's change in behavior, you can plan to eliminate the problem. If this proves impossible you may decide to allow the cat to live outside, but be sure you have a secure and sheltered place for him to stay in all kinds of weather. It's your responsibility to see to your cat's welfare outdoors as well as in.

Spraying

In a multi-cat household, sometimes a situation develops between cats that can lead to soiling problems. Perhaps one or more of the cats is marking his territory by putting his scent over the furniture or carpets. This is difficult to control.

If you have a "whole" male cat, in other words a tomcat that has not been neutered, please have him seen to. Neutered males are less likely to spray and you'll be helping to cut down on the unwanted cat population. Occasionally even females can spray.

If this problem arises, talk to your animals. Explain to them how much you love each of them, that they are part of the family and they need to share, both you and the territory where they live. Explain that it's unnecessary for them to mark their territory inside the house as all of it belongs to everyone. Explain how upsetting their spraying is. As you speak, visualize them spraying in the litter box.

Next, fill a spray bottle with water. When a cat is caught spraying, use the bottle to spray him back, preferably in the face. Soon he will associate the unpleasant sensation with his own spraying and the problem should diminish. Another idea is to place a bowl of food where the cat has sprayed or defecated. Cats seldom spray in an area where there is food.

Though these problem-solving routines require time and patience on the part of the human, they can often lead to a diminishing of, or even complete elimination of the problem. Cats are intelligent. They can be trained, but it must be done with patience and love.

$\mathcal{M}$ulti-Cat Household Problems

The three most common behavioral problems I encounter are soiling, spraying, and fighting. I am often able to trace the difficulty back to a drastic change, something that has upset the cat that has resulted in behavior which the human feels is inappropriate, but makes perfect sense to the feline.

It can take considerable research on my part to determine the reason and work out ways, with the owner, to correct the problem. With two or more cats in the family, problems can become extremely complex, particularly when a normal routine is turned upside down by introducing a new cat or cats into the household, as in the case of my clients Ann and Gordon.

$\mathcal{Z}$iggy and Yoda

Ann and Gordon had lived in harmony for four years with their perfectly well-behaved felines, Ziggy and Yoda, and then Ann became involved with a cat sanctuary called FLOCK (For the Love of Cats and Kittens) in Las Vegas.

An English lady called Sylvia Renee Lyss, who had been a professional dancer, started the shelter through her love of animals, especially cats and kittens. Sylvia now devotes her time to rescuing and feeding cats on the Las Vegas strip by night and working with the sanctuary during the day. All her money, time, and energy is spent in helping felines.

In July 1999, the worst storm in the Las Vegas area for a hundred years resulted in a raging river of water and mud that poured down from the mountains and raced through the sanctuary compound, sweeping away many cats outside at the time. A veterinarian technician risked his life to rescue cats and kittens submerged in mud and trapped against the fence.

When the media disclosed this horrifyingly sad story, many animal lovers' hearts went out to the plight of the cats. FLOCK is funded by donations from volunteers and the media coverage resulted in many people helping financially, as well as donating their time to care for the cats and kittens. As the shelter had been destroyed, foster homes were badly needed to care for many cats in shock. Unfortunately, the fence around the compound could not be replaced immediately and this made them easy prey for the coyotes. Some even ran into the desert. These cats had all been abandoned and they all deserved to have a better life.

Sadie and her brother Mikey had been abandoned in a motel room where Sadie gave birth to kittens. The sanctuary had rescued them. As all the FLOCK volunteers were busy rebuilding the sanctuary and fund-raising, anyone volunteering to provide a foster home was appreciated. Ann and Gordon helped by opening their hearts and home to a mother cat with five kittens. Ann had to keep her new cat family separated from Yoda and Ziggy as the rescued cats had ringworm.

Within two weeks, Ann had found a home for three of the kittens, leaving her trying to find homes for two older cats and two kittens. Ann had to turn down many of the prospective adopters, because most of them wanted to declaw the cats. Ann had no intention of allowing the cats to go to anyone that was likely to inflict this mutilation on any of the cats. She intended to keep the rest of her new cat family until the right homes were available. If she could not find loving homes for them, they would stay with her and Gordon.

After the new arrivals were spayed and neutered and were completely well, it was time for all the cats to learn to live together. After so many idyllic years, Ann and Gordon's fondest companions suddenly started to cause problems although they had tried to make sure Ziggy and Yoda felt loved and important.

The newcomers were a big annoyance to both of them, behaving badly in their opinion, and so, for the first time, Ziggy and Yoda also misbehaved. This was very distressing for Ann, as her house was being used as a giant litter box. Not only were the carpets destroyed, but also the cats were spraying on the sofas and other furniture and one was urinating on the bed. Moreover, Sadie and Ziggy were having fur-flying fights.

Ann could no longer live with the carpet or the unpleasant smell. She had the carpet replaced with tiles throughout the house. By the time she called me, she had put Ziggy and Yoda in her bedroom away from the others. She had also given Mikey the laundry room where he had his bed and a cat door leading into the courtyard.

I knew this was going to take more than one consultation as

there were so many problems, and follow-ups would be required if all the problems were going to be resolved. I always find that cats have good reasons for their accidents. Usually this is a way of communicating their displeasure with a particular situation that has developed at home.

Even small changes can throw cats completely. In this case, each cat wanted more territory and began putting his scent everywhere he could, as often as he could. That way, each cat's scent would remain strong, and the other cats would know to stay away. When the new cats came into the house, each brought its own scent. Ziggy and Yoda were used to each other's scents and their humans' scents, but the new cats' scents made the whole house smell unfamiliar.

So Ziggy and Yoda began spraying all over the house to try to restore its original smell. They did not understand how unpleasant the urine smell was to their human companions, since what smells nice to a cat doesn't smell nice to a human, and vice versa. As I tuned in to Ziggy and Yoda, I explained that I understood why they were marking their territory, but it was best to mark in the litter box. I also said they were making their human mother very unhappy, because humans cannot live with cat urine all over the house. Again I reinforced the idea of using the litter boxes as they had before the other cats arrived. I told them it was okay for the house to smell as it did now, with all the other cats' new scents.

Ann had left Yoda and Ziggy's litter boxes in her bedroom, so the other cats didn't use them. They told me they were happy about that, as they were *their* litter boxes. I asked them again to

use only the litter boxes in the bedroom and not to spray or urinate there, as Gordon and Ann were upset since the room was
special for all four of them. They told me they would not, if all
the other cats stayed out of the room. I explained that Ann
would keep them out. I felt their approval and sensed that they
would understand that taking care of their room meant they
should use the litter boxes at all times. I explained the bed was
just for sleeping on. They quickly informed me they had their
own blanket on the bed and the other cats did not sleep there.
This pleased them.

Ann decided to let Ziggy and Yoda out into the rest of the
house when she was at home and could watch them, since in the
past they had had the run of the house, and she felt that keeping
them shut in the bedroom was unacceptable on a long-term
basis. I explained this to Yoda and Ziggy and they agreed this
freedom was what they would like. I also thanked Ziggy and
Yoda for helping Ann to take care of the kittens. They informed
me they quite liked Rocky and Squirt, but they didn't want them
in their room. I told them that any time Rocky or Squirt came
into their room they could ask them to leave. They informed me
that they most certainly would.

I told Sadie, Rocky, and Squirt that they could use the other
bedroom where their litter boxes were, but that the main bedroom was Ziggy and Yoda's territory.

Then I asked Ziggy why she picked fights with Sadie. Suddenly
I could feel a sensation in my nose as Ziggy said it was because she
could not stand the way Sadie smelt. Her scent was disgusting and
it was all through the house. Ann agreed that Sadie did have a very

strong smell. I suggested to Ann she bathe Sadie each week. If the smell were not as strong, Ziggy would no longer pick fights with Sadie. Ann said she had taken Sadie to the vet because she was so aggressive, and the vet had given her pills to calm her down, but that hadn't helped since it was Ziggy who was picking the fights.

A few weeks later, Ann rang again, pleased because the fighting had stopped. She now bathes Sadie weekly and her strong scent has gone. Furthermore, Ziggy and Yoda no longer urinate in the bedroom. They use the litter boxes and when the felines are occupying the bedroom, they no longer relieve themselves outside the litter boxes.

The cats had their own reasons why they were using the bedroom as their giant litter box. They wanted the room to smell of their own scent only and those of their human companions so, by keeping the other cats out of *their* bedroom, the problem had been solved for both felines and humans.

However, Ziggy and Yoda still objected to the other cats' scents throughout the rest of the house. I suggested that Ann remove the rug for a while, as it held scent. The new tiles would not retain smells in the same way.

Cats do have their peculiarities. Ziggy and Yoda had not wished to use the other cats' litter boxes but wanted to put *their* scent all over the other cats' litter boxes, making a territorial statement to the other cats. By urinating on the rug and the litter boxes, they were letting the new arrivals know that their scents were still too strong throughout the house. By removing the rug, Ann had removed one of the problem areas.

I told Ziggy and Yoda I understood why they had been

spraying. When you speak to cats, you must always acknowledge what they are doing before you ask them to stop the behavior. Spraying on the other cats' litter boxes made perfect sense to Ziggy and Yoda. I asked, if they had to spray, could they please get into the litter box, rather than spray on the outside. I reminded them how much Ann loved them and also asked them if they could show the kittens, Squirt and Rocky, how to use the litter box properly, by getting in the box right away. I reminded them I was sure Ann would give them tuna fish if they could help to show the kittens the correct way to use the litter box.

I also asked Ann if she could provide a bit more quality attention to Ziggy and Yoda by making sure she went down on the floor to their level, or by bringing them into her lap to pet and talk to them. I suggested it was good to put a soft blanket on her lap, so the cats had something soft to knead.

I thanked both Ziggy and Yoda for talking to me, and then brought in Sadie, the mother cat, to tell her how kind she was to allow Ziggy and Yoda to help her look after her kittens. I could feel all the cats in harmony after speaking with them.

Ann called a month later to tell me there had been a great improvement with all the cats and they were rubbing along together. I congratulated Ann and Gordon, true animal lovers, who dealt with their felines' problems with compassion and understanding. Tolerance and patience won through in the end.

Here's an environmentally friendly way to remove the smell of cat urine:

1. Boil 2 cups water.

2. Add 1 cup baking soda.

3. Allow to cool.

4. Add 2 cups vinegar.

5. Put in a spray bottle. Shake well before each use.

6. Spray on urine spots while they're still wet, if possible.

7. Blot with towel/paper. Spray again. Blot dry.

8. Keep repeating.

Try not to get aggressive or irritable when this kind of problem occurs. I know that's asking for quite a lot of restraint, but understand that your cat is doing this because he is feeling insecure. Getting angry only adds to the cat's feeling of insecurity.

Whiskey

Janet is the human companion to eight cats. One day she returned from a business trip to find one of them had urinated on her pillow. She called me for advice. Before getting in touch with the cats, I explained to Janet that this was a way of marking territory and is a common problem. She told me Whiskey usually slept near her pillow.

When I connected telepathically with him, he was very annoyed because while Janet had been away another cat had slept on "his" pillow. Since he was in charge of the other cats and looked after his mummy at night, he had been upset to have the other cat's scent so near. We acknowledged he'd urinated on the pillow. I told him it upset Janet and to please not do it again. I suggested Janet put his food bowl on the pillow for a week as cats are quite clean and don't like to defecate and urinate where they eat. I also suggested she place a litter box on the area of the bed where Whiskey had urinated and gradually move the litter tray from that spot toward the edge of the bed and then move it down to the floor. If getting a new litter box, get one of the same color. Always use the same litter, preferably not a scented one. I know moving the box this way is inconvenient but I have found this to work well with cats that urinate on a bed. Employ this technique as soon as the problem occurs.

A month later Janet called to say she'd had no more problems with Whiskey urinating on the bed, but she was leaving on another business trip. Would I speak to Whiskey and ask him not to soil on the bed while she was away?

I advised her not to think of, or visualize, Whiskey urinating on the bed but to always see him urinating in the litter box as cats pick up on our thoughts. Always see what you want the cat to do, not what you *don't* want him to do. If you think, "I hope he will not urinate on the bed" he will receive the picture from your mind and get the wrong signal and perversely do just what you don't want him to do.

Always have positive thoughts and visualize good behavior. He will receive this positive message from you and understand.

I also suggested to Janet that she leave a T-shirt or old towel she'd used on other parts of the bed so the other cats could find her scent without going too near the pillow. I connected to Whiskey's feline companions and told them Janet was going to leave something special for them to sleep on and they were not to go near Whiskey's pillow. Janet reported after she returned from the trip that all was well.

Another bed problem was solved when I discovered the woman calling me had a new boyfriend who had recently been sleeping in her bed. He shut the cat that had been sleeping on his mum's bed for three years, out of the room. The cat was angered and did what any of us would have done if we were a cat— he marked his territory by defecating and urinating on *his* place in the bed.

I suggested the boyfriend feed the cat and give him treats when he visited and, of course, give him his old place back on the bed. I also communicated to the cat how kind he was to allow this man in his mum's bed and how sorry Mum was. Two weeks later the woman called back to tell me there were no more problems.

Skeeter

Quite often, what seems objectionable and inexplicable to us may make perfect sense to a feline. That was the case with Skeeter, owned by Fiona, who'd rescued twenty-five cats, many of whom slept with her and her cat-loving husband.

When I connected with the cats, Skeeter told me he had been with his human companion a long time. They had just taken away his blue bed covers—his favorite color—and the new ones smelled funny and didn't feel the same. He also resented the intrusion of all the other cats and especially some kittens his mum had just rescued. They were bothersome and jumped on the bed. He considered the bed his private territory.

I suggested Fiona put back the old sheets and bed covers or buy new blue ones as yellow upset Skeeter. I also advised her to keep the kittens out of the bedroom. I told her Skeeter was elderly and set in his ways and knew of no other way of voicing his displeasure to his humans than urinating on the bed.

Teapot

Yvonne and Teapot lived together happily for a number of years. Then Yvonne fell in love. Her partner had a little girl and they became a family. Yvonne and Teapot moved in to her partner's house and Teapot's litter box problems began. As I tuned into Teapot, he told me his mum still told him he was the most special love of her life and no one would ever take his place.

He told me the new house was very different with lots more room. (He and Yvonne had lived for nearly six years in a one-bedroom apartment.) But he also said that his new daddy had never lived with a cat before and he complained that Teapot was shedding hair all over the house. Teapot was indignant and told me his new daddy's hair came out even more than his did!

Yvonne laughed and confirmed this. Teapot also told me he had hair the same color as his mummy and he thought she was very beautiful.

I was then informed that Mummy had bought Teapot a new litter box and that this was constantly being moved around the house. He also said the new box was a different color and he liked the old color—blue. Some cats do not like any changes. The move to another home plus the new litter box of a different color upset Teapot. Nothing was familiar to him. It was also disturbing that the litter box was moved so often.

I told Yvonne to keep him in a small space for a time and leave his litter box in the same place and get him a blue one, since he liked that color. When making a change of this kind, it is always good to leave the old litter box beside the new one until the cat becomes used to the look and smell of the new box. Contrary to what some people may believe, cats *do* see color. They always remember the color of their first litter box. Their minds are sharp and so are their memories.

After explaining the situation to Yvonne, I told Teapot we understood how he felt, that his mummy was sorry and would give him back his blue litter box. Yvonne said she would also give him his own special room. Teapot was intrigued.

A few weeks later, I received another call from Yvonne telling me that Teapot was again refusing to use his litter box. When I tuned into Teapot, he sent me a picture of the box surrounded by furniture. Also, the box was at an angle and he didn't like that. It felt funny when he climbed inside.

Yvonne confirmed all this and told me his bedroom was

being used to store furniture. The litter box had been placed at an odd angle in the corner and sandwiched between several pieces of furniture. This made Teapot uncomfortable because he was afraid something would fall on him while he was in the box. Yvonne went home and cleared the furniture away and straightened the litter box. At once, everything returned to normal.

Many situations involving change can be traumatic for a feline. A move to a new home, a change of litter or litter box, a new human in their life or a favorite human no longer a part of their life—all can lead to problems. Yvonne did the right thing by assuring Teapot of his importance in her life, and sharing her thoughts with him. It helped him feel more secure even though all the familiar things around him were changing.

It took only a few final things, like straightening the litter box and removing the tall furniture, to get Teapot back using his litter box regularly.

A case was presented to me by two sisters who live with their cat, Dinky. They came to my office with Dinky in his crate. Sometimes clients like to bring their animals to meet me and sometimes they just bring a photograph.

Dinky was quite an outgoing cat and as I opened up his crate he walked out and informed me he was very pleased to be here and where was the cat that was going to be talking to him? I told him I was going to be talking to him and I was a cat whenever I spoke to cats. He accepted this and asked if his two human companions could stay home with him and never leave him in the house alone.

Pat and Linda said I should ask him why he wanted them home all the time because, whenever they left Dinky alone, they had big problems. When they were around he would always use the litter box and was quite good and clean, but when they left him alone, he used the house as if it were a giant litter box. When I asked Dinky why he did this I felt a tremendous fear. He told me he had not always used the rest of the house but had usually used his blue litter box. The ladies agreed. For the first nine months he always used the litter box.

Connecting back to Dinky, I realized he'd had a tremendous fright while still young. Both women were away from the house when Dinky went into the laundry room to use his litter box. As he was entering the box, he heard loud bangs outside the kitchen and saw bright lights outside. The noise kept on and on and the lights were very bright and moving. I knew this was not a thunderstorm. Dinky associated this terrifying noise with two incidents. When his human companions were in the house, he felt it was safe to use the litter box. But when he was left alone, Dinky was fearful that the flashing lights and noise would return if he used it.

Then Dinky sent me a picture of two teenage boys. The women confirmed they had neighbors with such sons. I told them the picture Dinky sent me looked like fireworks and asked if the boys had had fireworks while they were around. They were amazed and said yes, from time to time, the boys did set off firecrackers in the back yard. I knew this must be the cause of Dinky not using his litter box when he was alone. I asked if it were possible that the boys had thrown firecrackers into their yard near their kitchen. Pat said this was entirely possible.

I told Dinky that it was all right and that it was not likely to happen again. I told him the firecrackers could not hurt him while he was in the house. To give Dinky security and a sense of control and empowerment, I asked him where he would like his litter tray. He said he would prefer it upstairs in the closet in the bedroom he slept in.

Pat answered, "That's my room. He always sleeps on the bed with me and is often in the bedroom during the day." The sisters now understood why Dinky's problem had occurred and they were getting ready to leave when Dinky asked me if he could have more tuna as they had not given it to him for a while.

The sisters laughed and said they would serve him tuna or tinned mackerel or salmon once a week if he used his litter box all the time. He informed me that, if his request was met, he would accept these terms!

A week later I heard that Dinky had used his litter box consistently since the time they had gone home and the house was now a more pleasant place for all to live in.

Jasper

Carol had booked a telephone consultation. Her beautiful Siamese cat Jasper was a mature eighteen years old and had been frequently defecating outside his litter box. On top of that, for some reason unknown to Carol, he was constantly meowing.

Carol was very upset. Jasper's cries had increased dramatically, and she was afraid the noise would upset her neighbors. Besides that, he was keeping her from sleeping at night.

As I tuned in to Jasper, he told me he did go outside his litter box sometimes because the floor there smelled strongly of disinfectant. Carol told me the floor cleaner she used had a strong lemony smell. I explained that cats smell 2,000 percent more than we humans, so what smelled nice to her was quite objectionable to Jasper. The chemical smell on the floor was unbearable and was burning his sensitive nostrils.

Some household chemicals can be toxic to cats. I have known felines to become very ill from all the household sprays, disinfectant bleach products, and pesticides used in the house. I urge my clients to use vinegar and water for cleaning, as this is harmless. I explained to Carol that Jasper said the laundry near his litter box sometimes smelled bad, and this was another reason why he was using the carpet. She understood and said she would try to keep this from happening.

Then Jasper went on to tell me that he was Carol's cat and that his dad had walked out and left them both and that he did not come back to see Jasper. Carol confirmed that she was now divorced. I told her that Jasper was devastated.

Jasper said the smells in the new apartment were different and he didn't like them. He missed his dad's scent. All his life he had lived with the scent of these two human companions. One of the reasons he was crying so much was because the scent of his "father" human companion was no longer there. The only way he could explain his predicament to Carol was to cry loudly.

I asked Carol if she happened to have any shoes or old clothes from her ex-husband or could she ask him for an old shirt that had his scent on it. She said she had some of his clothes in the garage. I told her to put the shoes and clothes someplace in a closet but to put a shirt in Jasper's basket. A week later, Carol called to tell me that Jasper was back to his normal contented self. He was no longer crying dejectedly. And, at last, she could sleep through the night.

Her Royal Highness

Carol arrived with a three-year-old child under one arm and her problem cat, Princess, under the other.

Princess and Carol had lived together for eight years, so human and feline had shared many emotional traumas. Carol's marriage, now dissolved, had produced a beautiful daughter, Nicole, who loved Princess and was very gentle with her. Princess made herself comfortable and, feeling very much at ease, she informed me she was now ready to talk. She looked into my eyes and was extremely poised and confident. I did not have to ask her any questions.

Princess informed me that she knew I could speak her language. I found her to be a very chatty cat. She began by telling me about her hair falling out. She said it had been very upsetting for her but it had all grown back. She gave details of how she felt while experiencing this terrible ordeal. Carol said she had been quite stressed during her pregnancy with Nicole. Princess had been aware of Carol's emotional state. By tuning in to Carol's feelings and emotions, Princess had taken on her human companion's worries and had also become stressed. This had resulted in her hair loss.

I informed Princess that this had sometimes happened to other cats when their human companions were pregnant. By telling Princess this, I made her feel she was not alone. I said she was beautiful and her hair was now thick and glossy. She again told me she knew she was beautiful but she liked me to tell her anyway. As I was talking with Princess, I could tell she lived with another feline. Carol said this was correct. His name was Charlie. I acknowledged him and could tell he was a laid-back cat. He told me he adored Princess.

Princess jumped into the conversation to say she would tell me anything I wanted to know about Charlie. She said I shouldn't waste my time talking to him, since she was the one having the consultation. I could feel Charlie withdraw immediately. I thanked him for talking to me and continued the conversation with Her Royal Highness!

Princess, this very sensitive feline, continued talking and telling me that Carol had a new man in her life. Princess liked him. I told Carol this was a big plus since some cats can become very jealous when a new boyfriend comes into the domestic scene. Carol said any new boyfriend would have to love cats, otherwise she would not continue the relationship as Princess was her child too.

Then Princess told me she urinated on the sofa and carpet. I asked her why. Carol had told me this was the first time in six years that Princess had not used her litter box. Then Princess showed me pictures of two small children screaming and running after her and even following her into what she thought was her safe haven, under the bed in the master bedroom. The children grabbed at her, pulling her fur. Princess found it frightening. She had nowhere else to escape.

Carol said the children were her new boyfriend's and they had chased Princess, but she had stopped them. I reminded Carol that with three small children running around you needed eyes in the back of your head. I told her she would have to protect Princess from them, otherwise she would continue to urinate all over the house.

I suggested Carol lock Princess in the bedroom with her litter box and food and water bowls, whenever the children were coming. That would make her feel safe. No matter how severe the problem, the resolution can be found once the cause has been found. Usually the cat's behavioral change has to do with a change in human conduct. In this case, Princess's environment had been invaded and her usually good behavior pattern had suffered.

In this chapter, we have discussed some reasons why felines soil outside their litter boxes. If you have such a problem with your cat always try to examine the problem from the feline's perspective, not just from your own. By doing so you should be able to reach a happy conclusion for the both of you.

Chapter Eight

Healthy Diet and Nutrition

"Food has a threefold purpose for the consumer:
to nourish, to induce growth, and to give health protection."
—JULIETTE DE BAIRACLI LEVY[1]

YOU probably thought hard about bringing a cat into your home, considering the lifelong commitment to your newest family member very carefully. You've read up on diet, exercise, and vaccinations, researched breeds, and discussed the decision with family and friends.

The pet-care industry is booming but before you race out to stock up on cat food and flea control products and schedule vet visits, I would like to discuss traditional pet-care theories—where they are beneficial and where they fall short. There is now a growing acceptance of alternative diet, maintenance, and

---

[1] 1. de Baïracli Levy, Juliette, *The Complete Herbal Handbook for the Dog and Cat,* Faber and Faber, 1992, p. 4.

care for your feline friend. Many ideas are worth evaluating in your plans to give your cat as healthy a life and environment as possible.

$\mathscr{P}$et Foods

The first commercial pet food was a dog biscuit introduced in England in 1860. An American electrician, James Spratt, was working in London when he saw dogs being fed leftover biscuits from docked ships. He decided to devise a version of biscuits made with wheat meals, vegetables, beetroot and meat.

The combination found favor throughout England with sporting dogs, and in 1890, Spratt's formula went public and production began in the United States where formulations of fortified biscuits and dry cat food entered the market. In the 1930s, canned horsemeat was introduced as a food for dogs, and canned cat food and dry meat-meal dog foods followed. By the 1950s and 1960s, dry cat food was available as well as varieties of canned products, and soft-moist food products.

These developments were born out of convenience and commercialism as a way to meet the growing pet population. Although one assumes that no harm was intended in the creation of these diets, harm has come in a variety of forms because they have moved dogs and cats away from their natural raw food diets. Dogs and cats have been domesticated for centuries, but before the days of commercial food, they foraged for food or ate, like their owners, combinations of meat, grains, and vegetables.

According to the American Pet Products Manufacturers Association[2], in the United States, 62 percent of all households own a pet, ranging from dogs, cats, and rabbits to more exotic snakes and spiders. Dogs and cats have been the most popular American pets and their population in 2001 reached just over 141 million, with 40 million households owning dogs and almost 35 million owning cats.

Those numbers, combined with the European pet population of 47 million cats and 41 million dogs, and the UK population of almost 8 million cats and 6 million dogs, explain why the pet-food industry has hit $25 billion worldwide, with $7 billion of those sales in the United States.

According to the Animal Protection Institute of America (APIA), the idea that one pet food can provide all the nutrition a companion animal will ever need for his entire life is a "myth."[3] The APIA says cereal grains are the primary ingredients in most commercial foods, providing today's cats and dogs with "a primarily carbohydrate diet with little variety that is a far cry from the primary proteins with lots of variety that their ancestors ate."[4]

Any responsible pet owner will try to understand what the labels on pet food do and don't tell you. If you look at a bag of regular-grade dry cat food from the local grocer, two of the top three ingredients are commonly some type of grain, often corn.

---

[2] *Pet Industry Facts*, American Pet Products Manufacturers' Association, <http://www.appma.org/press/fact_sheet_03.asp>
[3] *What's Really in Pet Food*, Animal Protection Institute, February 23, 2001, <http://www.api4animals.org/doc.asp?ID=79>
[4] Ibid.

Even though cats are carnivores that must eat meat to fulfill physiological needs, the pet food industry plies them with corn. One reason must be cost.

Processed pet food also often contains soybeans, which are not easily digestible and are often a source of allergies in cats and dogs. They often occur in pet food as "fiber content." What makes the soybean doubly useless as a food source in dry pet food is its exposure to high temperatures during preparation, whereby its nutritional value is rendered nil.

According to Paws-itive Choice, a family-run holistic animal care business in Canada, fiber percentage listed as processed pet food can also include "vegetable fiber" (peanut hulls, corn husks) or "cellulose," which is largely indigestible to dogs and can by law actually be blood-soaked sawdust from slaughterhouse floors.[5] The company adds that "beet pulp," another common pet-food ingredient with no nutritional value, is actually an artificial stool hardener, preventing diarrhea, and the body's natural reaction to unhealthy foods. If a pet food includes grains, Paws-itive Choice says it's important that those grains be designated as "whole," since "hulls, mill run and grain by-products are the cheap waste product of the human food industry after the nutritious parts have been extracted."[6]

Nonfood preservatives found in regular-grade commercial pet food include chemicals such as butylated hydroxyanisole, butylated hydroxtoluene, and ethoxyquin, which have been

---

[5] *Evaluating Pet Food*, Paws-itive Choice, February 23, 2001, <http://www.pawsitive choice.com/evaluate.htm>

[6] Ibid.

linked to behavioral problems as well as cancer, brain, and liver damage. Ethoxyquin is a chemical additive intended for use by the rubber industry. The company that manufactures it has it labeled as a poison, the US Department of Agriculture says it is a pesticide, and it is actually banned in the use of human food but, so far, it has not been banned in pet foods.

Rancid oils or leftover restaurant oils can also be found in commercial pet food—it's the unique, pungent odor you encounter when you open a new bag of dry food—and it can include anything from recycled refined animal fat and kitchen grease to other oils considered unfit for humans. These fats and oils are sprayed on to dried food to make it palatable while also serving as a binding agent for other flavor enhancers.

When you get into protein labeling on commercially processed foods, it's important to understand where that protein originates. Ingredients that are simply tagged "poultry by-products" can actually include such viscera as the heart, lungs, and intestines as well as chicken feet and heads, duck beaks, feathers, and hides. Labels do not specify how clean those parts are when they are processed, or whether they are free from fecal content. These ingredients are not ideal for anyone's consumption, nor your pet's, and their hidden inclusion in pet food contributes to a variety of ailments that can affect their skin, the digestive tract, and general health.

Another scary statistic is the occurrence of cat and dog meat and bone ending up in pet food. Eatveg.com cites statistics that estimate that U.S. animal shelters euthanize 13 million household pets annually, with 30 percent buried, 30 percent cremated,

and 40 percent—almost 5.2 million—sent to rendering factories.[7] Those factories provide source materials to companies that
include pet-food manufacturers, although they commonly deny
any knowledge of those ingredients in their products.

In the United States the Pet Food Institute states in its guidelines that "pet food manufacturers have strict controls over their
supplies of proteins, from both slaughterhouses and renderers,
and only farm animals (the same animals used for human food)
are used in pet foods," but undercover investigators in Balti-
more, Maryland, discovered that the remains of household pets
do indeed find their way into pet food.[8] This occurs even though
renderers must legally swear that meal products do not include
household pets.

When commercial pet food manufacturers include livestock
in their products, Paws-itive Choice points out that it may not
necessarily be "human-grade" meat, but instead meat designated as "4d"—diseased, dying, disabled, or dead. It's a horrifying thought, and the potential contamination does not end
there. According to Paws-itive Choice, "4d meats are 'dena-
tured,' " sprayed with chemicals like kerosene to prevent them
from being sold as human grade and then cooked at extremely
high temperatures to be 'sterilized'." If dogs and cats have been
included in a pet-food source and they were euthanized with
sodium pentobarbital, the drug is also present in the end product because it survives the rendering process.[9]

---

[7] *Pet Food Alert!*, Eatveg.com, February 23, 2001, <http://www.eatveg.com/animals/petfood.htm>
[8] Ibid.
[9] *Evaluating Pet Food*, Paws-itive Choice, February 23, 2001, <http://www.pawsitivechoice.com/eval-uate.htm>

Ann Martin, in her book *Food Pets Die For: Shocking Facts about Pet Food* (NewSage Press), paints a disturbing portrait of what goes on in rendering plants. She writes that dead-stock removal operations play a major role in the industry, turning over road kill, even dead zoo animals, to renderers. She says when these animals are brought in, usable meat is removed from the carcass and then covered in charcoal to prevent it from being used for human consumption. From that point, it can be sold as "animal food," a tag that includes pet food.

In addition to the restaurant grease I mentioned earlier, Martin writes that garbage, as well as meats and baked goods from supermarkets (long past sell-by dates and with the Styrofoam trays and shrink wrap still attached) can be rendered in these plants, as can the entrails from dead stock removal operations and condemned and contaminated material from slaughterhouses. The heads, feet, skin, toenails, hair, feathers, carpal and tarsal joints, mammary glands, cancerous tissue or tumors, worm-infested organs, injection sites, blood clots, bone splinters, contaminated blood, stomach, and bowels of these animals can also be rendered. In addition, although the US Food and Drug Administration and the Environmental Protection Act prevent pesticides from being passed along in "human grade meat," Martin writes that carcasses containing high levels of drugs, pesticides, and contaminated material do find their way into pet food.[10]

In the United Kingdom, the Pet Food Manufacturers' Association (PFMA) guarantees that their members only use meat

---

[10] Excerpted online at http://www.homevet.com/petcare/foodbook.html

from animal species generally accepted in the human food chain—beef, lamb, pork, poultry, shellfish, fish, rabbit, and game—and only buy from reputable suppliers procuring from licensed United Kingdom and European Union slaughterhouses and poultry plants. Diseased and contaminated meat cannot legally be used in pet food—and this includes the bovine tissue believed to spread BSE, or Bovine Spongiform Encephalitis, more commonly known as Mad Cow Disease.[11]

Since the material used in pet food in the United Kingdom—both animal and cereal—comes from sources intended for human consumption, it is protected by the same EU and UK laws governing levels of pesticide and residue levels of veterinary substances meant to protect people. Of course, there has been much debate about whether these laws are stringent enough, and there has been concern about the levels of pesticide found on nonorganic food.

Unfortunately, chemical analysis does not address the palatability, digestibility, and biological availability of nutrients in pet food and is unreliable for determining whether a food will provide an animal with sufficient nutrients. Acknowledging these limitations, AAFCO added a "safety factor" to exceed the minimum amount of nutrients required in order to meet the complete and balanced requirements. The end result is that the pet-food industry has developed its own standards for nutritional adequacy.[12]

---

[11] www.pfma.com

[12] *What's Really in Pet Food*, Animal Protection Institute, February 23, 2001, <http://www.api4animals.org/doc.asp?ID=79>

Since the introduction of commercial pet-food alternatives, there have been increased instances of ailments attributable to poor nutrition. Dry commercial pet food can be contaminated with bacteria, which can cause acute vomiting and diarrhea. Urinary tract disease is one condition directly related to poor diet in both cats and dogs. Plugs, crystals, and stones in cat bladders are often caused by commercial pet food formulas. Manufactured cat foods have been altered in recent years to affect acidity in urine and the amount of some minerals has directly affected the development of urinary tract diseases. Dogs can also form stones as a result of their diet.

Taurine deficiency in commercial cat food was a leading cause of heart disease and blindness in cats and heart disease in some dogs. To rectify that, taurine is now a supplement of commercial diets, but it was only added after the health defects directly attributed to its absence were identified. The instances of hyperthyroidism in cats have risen since the 1970s and although the exact cause is unknown, it is believed that it is a side effect of lifelong poor nutrition resulting from a diet of commercial pet food. Other nutritional problems that occur with cereal-based pet foods are due to a variety of factors, including the fact that it's an incomplete diet which can include additives, bacteria, toxins, and other organisms.

Since these disturbing correlations between poor diet and poor or substandard health, there has been a move in recent years to offer an alternative to dry and canned food. The first step has been the introduction of high-grade and prescription pet foods to the marketplace. These superior foods, while still commercially processed, utilize better protein and grain sources in a more healthy balance and tend to include natural additives and supplements rather than low-grade meat and grains and chemicals and secondhand by-products. While the high-grade cat food and wet food diets on the market are an improvement on the low-grade foods, don't just buy on reputation. It's still a very good idea to read the labels thoroughly, and visit vendor websites for detailed information about the ingredients in their products.

The other alternative to low-grade commercial pet food, the "raw" diet plan, is supported by a number of holistic practitioners who offer specific instructions on creating a balanced, healthy raw food alternative for your animal. Joel Hyman, a holistic practitioner and master herbalist, has given me permission to reprint his fabulous natural diet for cats and dogs. This can also be used as a guide for developing your pet's diet:

Joel Hyman's Natural Fresh Food Diet for Cats and Dogs

First, it's best to feed your animal twice daily, with one feeding in the morning and one in the evening. (If you have an animal with a medical condition that requires the all-day availability of food, you can of course supplement this diet with a high-grade cat food or feed in smaller meals throughout the day.)

One part raw meat and fish

Medium dogs usually eat 3–4 ounces per meal—adjust this accordingly for larger and smaller animals. Lamb is the best protein source for medium and larger dogs. For toy or miniature dogs or cats, rabbit or poultry is best.

If the meat is frozen or refrigerated, freshen it in boiling water for 2–3 minutes first. Put one handful of salt in a bowl of tepid water and place the freshened or fresh meat or fish in the solution for 14 minutes to eliminate parasites. Rinse well. Liver and other organs (i.e. kidneys, brains, etc.) should be fed no more than two times a week. Bones: soft bones are best fed (i.e. ribs or flat bones) *after meals,* with meat still left on them.

Cereals

Cereals are a good source of vitamins and minerals. Give only 1–2 times weekly. Use oats (flaked), barley (flaked), or rye (whole grain), which is low in fat and good for overweight dogs. These grains can often be found in bulk at local health-food stores. Corn (grated or mashed and never fed in excess) is a glandular tonic and good for your animal's hair. You can also give canned creamed corn as a treat every once in a while. Brown rice and mashed beans are also good cereal sources.

Vegetables

Vegetables (raw, grated fine, or in a food processor) are a good source for alkali. Carrots (raw, finely grated) are good blood cleansers. You can also give broccoli, peppers, squash, and raw, mashed avocado. Tahini can also be given—2 teaspoons, 3 times weekly. This is not an exclusive list—experiment with other vegetables as well and see which your animal takes to.

Cheese

It's best to only feed your animal white cheeses. Cottage cheese is very good. Non-white cheeses are usually artificially colored and are best left out of your pet's diet.

Fruit

Grapes, berries, melons, coconut, and apples are all good for your animal.

Nuts

It's best to feed your animal ground nuts: pine nuts, almonds, walnuts, and filberts are all good choices. Use only natural, raw, or unsalted nuts. Loose nuts from your grocer or health-food store are best, as canned nuts are often highly salted and full of preservatives.

Eggs

Eggs are a good source of protein. One day a week, give your animal two raw eggs, with vegetables and/or fruit.

Water

Always give your animal purified water, as tap water can contain harsh metals. Preferably, to aid in food digestion, you should not allow your animal to drink immediately after meals, however water should be available and accessible at all times. Give your animal fresh water daily, never give them milk.

The above foods should be given at the following ratios to appropriately balance acidic and alkaline properties for good digestion:

> *Protein = 60–70% of meal (acid salt)*
> *Fruit and vegetables = 30–40% of meal (alkaline)*

When you take your pet off processed canned or dry food, it is best to wean him gradually and not to stop his old diet abruptly:

- The first week, give your pet one feeding of the old diet and one feeding of the fresh food diet per day.

- The second week, give him five servings of the old diet with nine per week of the new.

- The third week, give him three feedings of the old diet and eleven of the new.

- By the fourth week, he is completely off of the processed food and solely on a fresh food natural diet.

General

Meat should be given 4 to 6 days per week.

Meatless days are 1 to 2 days per week (egg, cheese, etc.).

Add a daily multivitamin and vitamin C with rose hip syrup (large dog = 1,000 mg daily and scale down according to animal size). Give once daily with food. Scale back on the amount of vitamin C you give your animal if you notice the development of loose stools or diarrhea, and reintroduce at a lesser dosage.

Exposure to sunlight is good (but not for extended periods of time, as animals are prone to skin cancers just as humans are). Spray coat (with a nontoxic spray or all-natural citronella spray) and groom for fleas, ticks, and mites once a week.

As a general rule of thumb, I always say that I will not give my animals food I would not eat myself. I use Joel's diet with my animals and they thrive on it. Some of my cats will eat raw foods, while the others like their fish and meat cooked. Two of them love cantaloupe and raisins. They all enjoy cottage cheese and yogurt and all of my animals love omelets. An omelet once a week does no harm.

Water

As Joel points out, it is best to give your cat purified water. Spring water is best. You can buy bottled water, or install a filter that you can use for everyone's drinking water.

If you give your cat treats, make sure they are natural snacks of dried fruits or vegetables rather than processed biscuits. My cats love dried apricots and nuts.

Other Natural Diets

There are a variety of other sources on the market offering advice for this type of diet. Dr Richard Pitcairn, in his book, *Dr. Pitcairn's Complete Guide to Natural Health for Dogs and Cats* (Rodale Press), recommends several raw food diet combinations that address specific health conditions in dogs and cats as well as general health. Juliette de Baïracli Levy, a holistic advocate in the United Kingdom and author of *The Complete Herbal Handbook for the Dog and Cat* (Faber and Faber), suggests raw food as a remedy for almost anything that ails our companion animal population.

She cites several cases of improved and restored health in dogs and cats based on a raw food diet and also believes that pet ailments now accepted as common did not exist when animals foraged and killed for what they ate. She suggests that the new reliance on prepared foods has diminished their natural immunity to disease and infection. She proposes diet combinations for specific ailments and for general health.

Yet another widely read book on alternative therapies, *Four Paws Five Directions: A Guide to Chinese Medicine for Cats and Dogs* (Celestial Arts) by Dr. Cheryl Schwartz, proposes a raw food diet as part of a natural lifestyle for companion animals. Dr. Martin Goldstein's book, *The Nature of Animal Healing* (Alfred

A. Knopf), is a must-read for all animal lovers. Dr. Goldstein's book features a section on animal nutrition and branded food products.

All of these books are ideal places to start your research. Before you think that the daily preparation of a raw food or natural food diet is too much trouble, think again. It's entirely possible to work raw food for your pets into your scheduled routine without taking much time. It may seem daunting at first to build a diet for your animals from scratch but the end results are well worth your small extra effort and you will see such a difference in your pet.

As Joel Hyman advises, if you are introducing the diet to an older animal who has been used to dry cat food or canned meat, introduce the raw food diet gradually, as sudden changes could cause an initial upset to the digestive system. Most animals take to raw diets immediately. In some instances, you may have to begin with cooked meat and scale back to raw for animals who have had that instinct for raw flesh muted. If you begin right away with a new puppy or kitten, you are establishing a wonderful routine.

When shopping for raw food you can save time and money by buying meat and grains in bulk and preparing "batch" meals and storing them in the refrigerator or freezer, thawing or letting settle to room temperature at feeding time. It's best to not feed a raw diet too cold, as it can inhibit proper digestion.

$\mathcal{V}$accinations

Another area of traditional animal care is yearly vaccinations. Some vets, however, have betrayed the owner's wish to safeguard his animal's health and actually endangered it by recommending too many vaccinations. Recent research has proven that yearly jabs are not actually necessary for all diseases. While laws in some parts of the world require yearly vaccinations, most of us need not worry about annual shots. Here I'll discuss what these vaccinations are and their risks, in which instances they are necessary, and how to vaccinate responsibly if you are bound by law to do so.

The immune system plays a vital role in your cat's health. One of the most important functions of this highly complex network of specialized cells and molecules is to protect cats from disease and infection caused by viruses, bacteria, and a host of other microbes and parasites intent on assaulting the body and causing disease.

"Vaccines are given to prepare the body's immune system against invasion by a particular disease-causing organism. Vaccines contain antigens, which to the immune system 'look' like the organism but don't, ideally, cause disease. When the vaccine is introduced by injection or some other means, the immune system responds by mounting a defense. When the cat is subsequently exposed to the organism, the immune system is prepared and either prevents infection or reduces the severity of disease."[13]

---

[13] *Feline Vaccines: Benefits and Risks*, Cornell Feline Health Center, February 26, 2001, <http://web.vet.cornell.edu/Public/FHC/vaccbr.html>

The American Association of Feline Practitioners recommends the following core vaccines for all cats: feline panleukopenia (distemper), feline viral rhinotracheitis, and feline calicivirus every three years, and rabies once a year.[14] While this study has found this vaccination schedule to be effective, keep in mind that the vaccine manufacturers recommend annual vaccinations for all the above named conditions. You and your vet must make the determination of a proper vaccination schedule for your feline, taking into account such variables as his age and health, whether he is an indoor or outdoor cat, potential exposure to other cats and local disease conditions.

According to expert authorities, the decision to vaccinate your cat is dependent on several factors, including:

• Your cat's risk of exposure to disease-causing organisms—this is dependent on the health of the other cats your cat is exposed to and the environment in which your cat lives.

• The consequence/severity of infection if not vaccinated.

• The risk an infected cat poses to human health.

• The protective ability of the vaccine.

• The frequency or severity of reactions the vaccine produces.

• The age and health of your cat.

---

[14] <http://www.peteducation.com/article.cfm?cls=1&cat=1385&articleid=951>

- Previous vaccine reactions your cat may have experienced.

You should begin by speaking to your vet about which vaccines you feel are appropriate for your cat based on the above criteria, and if he will not discuss limiting vaccines or altering vaccination cycles, find another vet.

The vaccines your cat can be given include the following.

Feline Panleukopenia Virus Vaccine:

Feline panleukopenia (feline distemper or FPV) is a highly contagious and deadly viral disease. It can survive extremes of temperature and humidity for many months, and is resistant to most disinfectants. Until recently, panleukopenia was the most serious infectious disease of cats, claiming the lives of thousands every year. Because of the highly effective vaccines currently available, panleukopenia is now considered rare. The AAFP and Cornell University in the United States caution, however, that because the disease is so serious and the presence of the virus continues in the environment, vaccination is recommended for all cats. A 1999 study published in the *American Journal of Veterinary Research* stated that these vaccinations maintain their antibodies for over three years and can be administered on a triennial basis.[15]

---

[15] Scott, Fred W., DVM, PhD, and Geissinger, Cordell M., BS, "Long-Term Immunity in Cats Vaccinated with an Inactivated Trivalent," *American Journal of Veterinary Research*, May 1999, Vol. 60, No. 5, reprinted online at <http://www.naturalholistic.com/nhpc/handouts/vaccines_7year.htm/>

Feline Viral Rhinotracheitis:

Feline viral rhinotracheitis causes upper respiratory infections and may cause a pregnant cat to abort her kittens. Unlike feline calicivirus and herpes virus organisms that are difficult to kill with normal household cleaning procedures, rhintotracheitis virus is quite susceptible to standard cleaning techniques, so vigilant attention to hygiene and isolation of symptomatic cats can go a long way toward containing any spread of this infection. The AJVR study stated that these vaccinations also maintain their antibodies for over three years and can be administered on a triennial basis.[16]

Feline Calicivirus/Herpes Virus Vaccine:

Feline calicivirus (FCV) and feline herpes virus type I (FHV) are responsible for most (80–90 percent) infectious feline upper respiratory tract diseases. Most cats are exposed to one or both of these viruses at some time. Once infected, many cats never completely rid their systems of it. These "carrier" cats can continuously or intermittently shed the organisms for long periods—perhaps for life—and are therefore a major source of infection to other cats. While the currently available vaccines minimize the severity of upper respiratory infections, none will prevent disease in all situations. The AJVR study stated that these vaccinations also maintain their antibodies for over three years and can be administered on a triennial basis.[17]

---

[16] Ibid.
[17] Ibid.

Rabies Virus Vaccine:

The rabies vaccine is required in the United States and other areas of the world where the disease can be epidemic in wildlife populations.

Feline Leukemia Virus Vaccine:

Feline leukemia virus (FeLV) is the leading viral killer of cats. It is spread from cat to cat through bite wounds, through casual contact with infected cats, and from an infected mother cat to her kittens. Most at risk are outdoor cats, indoor/outdoor cats, and cats exposed to them. Cats living in households with FeLV-infected cats or with cats of unknown infection status are also at risk. Indoor cats with no exposure to potentially infected cats are extremely unlikely to become infected. FeLV vaccines are recommended only for cats at risk of exposure to the virus.

Chlamydia, Feline Infectious Peritonitis, and Ringworm Vaccines

Vaccines are available for each of these disease-causing organisms, but their use is not routinely recommended for all cats. If your vet recommends these, ask him why before the vaccines are administered. The American Association of Feline Practitioners recommends these vaccines should only be used where the specific conditions are endemic or where husbandry conditions suggest there is a chance that any contagion has a higher likelihood of spreading due to close contact among cats.[18]

If you are planning to travel with your pet, discuss the necessary vaccinations for your country of origin and destination with your vet before you travel.

Now that you have an outline of what your cat is being vaccinated against, you need to understand that not all of these vaccines "expire" quickly and when you repeat them every year, you are not necessarily boosting the vaccine properties, but actually weakening your animal's immune system.

There are approved rabies vaccines that can be given every three years if your country or destination does not require yearly rabies vaccinations. Recent research "suggests that the panleukopenia/rhinotracheitis/calicivirus vaccines provide adequate protection for several years, so in response many veterinarians are now recommending that this vaccine be 'boosted' at three year intervals."[19] The duration of other vaccines has not been tested and you should consider annual vaccination according to your cat's risk of exposure.

You should be aware that side effects can result from some vaccines, including discomfort or irritation at the site where the shot was given, mild fever, diminished appetite and activity, sneezing four to seven days after administration of an intranasal jab, and the development of a small, firm, swelling under the skin at the site where the vaccine was given. This non-painful

---

[18] <http://www.peteducation.com/article.cfm?cls=1&cat=1385&articleid=951>
[19] *Feline Vaccines: Benefits and Risks*, Cornell Feline Health Center, February 26, 2001, <http://web.vet.cornell.edu/Public/FHC/vaccbr.html>

swelling usually subsides after several weeks, but you should alert your vet so he can record that your animal did have a reaction so he can keep an eye on the swelling.

In serious and rare cases, potentially life-threatening allergic reaction can occur within minutes of vaccination, or up to an hour later. In the last several years, the most recent and serious side effect of yearly vaccinations has been vaccination site sarcomas, where a tumorous growth occurs at the vaccination site. This can occur several weeks, months, or longer after a vaccination is given.

The AAFP and the Academy of Feline Medicine (AFM) recently issued its yearly feline vaccination guidelines, and it's important to note that right at the beginning of the document, the authors state, "Most vaccinations do not induce complete protection from infection or disease, nor do they induce the same degree of protection in all animals."[20] Immunizations are not an exact science, and it's important to understand that they are potentially a safeguard against disease but not an absolute guarantee that your animal will not get one of these diseases. Vaccinations simply dramatically decrease the likelihood of the disease occurring when they are administered responsibly.

Other considerations to keep in mind, according to Dr. Richard Pitcairn, are to minimize coordinating vaccinations with other vet activities, such as spay or neuter appointments, when your pet will be under anesthesia soon before or soon after vac-

---

[20] 2000 Report of the American Association of Feline Practitioners and Academy of Feline Medicine, *Advisory Panel on Feline Vaccines*, p.7. <http://www.aafponline.org/about/guidelines_vaccine.pdf>

cinations are administered. He writes, "The routine practice of giving vaccinations at the same time a pet is undergoing anesthesia or surgery . . . can introduce the vaccine organism at a time when the immune system is depressed for several weeks. It is equally unwise to use corticosteroids (to control skin itching, for instance) at the time of vaccination. The steroid acts to depress the immune response and disease resistance at the same time the vaccine challenges the body to respond vigorously to an introduced organism."[21]

Dr. Pitcairn adds that vaccines can also possibly cause an acute disease or chronic health problem. "I have often noticed certain animals getting ill a few days to a few weeks after receiving vaccinations," he writes. "In my opinion most of these instances are illness from the vaccine itself. It is likely that the animal was in a weakened state and the vaccine virus therefore caused a more severe reaction than the 'mini-disease' intended."[22]

Dr. Pitcairn cites this problem as occurring most often after vaccinations for canine distemper, canine parvovirus, feline rhinotracheitis, and feline calicivirus. He adds that the feline leukemia virus has, in his experience, created conditions that allowed for the occurrence of feline infectious peritonitis (FIP). "Sometimes the second virus was already in the cat, but the immune system was strong enough to withstand it until weakened by the vaccine disease."[23] The introduction of the vaccine was

---

[21] Pitcairn, Richard, DVM, *Dr. Pitcairn's Complete Guide to Natural Health for Dogs and Cats*, Rodale Press, 1995, p., 322.

[22] Ibid.

[23] Ibid, p. 323.

essentially then too much for the immune system to fight along with the preexisting but latent condition of FIP.

Finally, Dr. Pitcairn has found that when homeopathically treating animals, he must often remove the effects of vaccinations before being able to "make significant progress in the difficult, chronic cases that are often brought to me."[24]

His most serious condemnation of the damage that vaccines can do is wide ranging. "It is my opinion that most skin allergies (and similar skin diseases) are the result of repeated annual vaccinations," he writes. "I also suspect that the widespread increase in diseases caused by immune system disorders (such as hyperthyroidism, inflammatory bowel disease, lupus, and pemphigus) is a result of increased use of vaccinations, especially of combination formulas."[25]

Dr. Pitcairn suggests that the natural conditions by which an animal is normally exposed to pathogens from which its body is built to defend itself—via the nose, mouth, or other mucous membranes—is bypassed and essentially bombarded by the introduction of a vaccine's pathogens going straight into the bloodstream. Dr. Pitcairn's alternative to vaccinations is a homeopathic remedy called nosodes, which are derived from natural products. They were first developed as a means of inoculation in the 1920s and are now used by homeopathic vets. They are, however, not legally accepted as a vaccination substitute. Be aware that if you choose this route to immunize your pet and you

[24] Ibid, p. 323.
[25] Ibid.

are required by law to register and vaccinate your pet, you are not officially "covered."

Dr. Pitcairn's advice if you must resort to vaccinations is to inoculate against one disease at a time. If your vet will not offer single-disease vaccinations, he advises that you request simpler combined vaccinations such as a combination hepatitis and distemper for dogs and a 3-in-1 panleukopenia, rhinotracheitis, and calicivirus for cats. He advises that these are much better than "mega-mix" shots that combine several vaccines in one cocktail. He also suggests that you request "killed" or inactive vaccines that cannot grow in the body. For many years the use of vaccines developed using strains of inactive, weakened or dead virus for both human and animal use has been a common feature in many branches of medicine and is now even used in the treatment of AIDS. The process of introducing these vaccines into the body is designed to kick-start the immune system into producing antibodies and creating a resistance to infection in case of attack from a live virus.

Dr. Pitcairn advises that vaccinations should only be administered after your pet reaches sixteen weeks. For timed vaccinations of puppies, he advises shots at twenty-two weeks or older. In his opinion, only distemper and parvo are essential for dogs. For cats, Dr. Pitcairn feels that a feline panleukopenia vaccination is good for the life of the cat after the vaccination at sixteen weeks. While he generally does not recommend rhinotracheitis and calicivirus inoculations for cats, he does support the 3-in-1 vaccination if there are no available alternatives. He feels strongly that feline leukemia is the most harmful of all cat vaccines available. He warns that cats are more prone to latent virus activation via their over-vaccination.

It's extremely important that when you vaccinate, you evaluate your animal's overall health—an animal that is ill or has a secondary condition or congenital ailment may not be healthy enough to cope. Discuss this with your vet. If you are dealing with chronic conditions and you are required by law to inoculate at some point, discuss your options with your vet, and again, if your vet is unresponsive, find another one.

It's important for me to clarify here that should you choose to err on the side of caution and scale back on annual vaccinations, do not, by any means, discontinue annual checkups for your animals. A vet is a repository of a wealth of experience and expertise and can be very wise in evaluating your pet's health. An annual checkup involving an examination of your animal's heart, lungs, chest, abdomen, eyes, ears, and mouth, and a yearly blood profile, can tell you exactly how your animal is doing and head off any health conditions that may be developing. Regardless of your vaccination schedule, an annual checkup is part of being a responsible pet parent. In older animals, a visit twice yearly is recommended.

Vitamins, Supplements, and Alternative Therapies

You may have been surprised to see the inclusion of vitamins and supplements in Joel Hyman's remarks earlier. Just as vitamins and supplements help human systems, they have the same effect on animals. Herbs and homeopathic remedies have a place in the well-being of animals too. The aforementioned books by Dr. Schwartz, Ms. de Baïracli Levy and Dr. Pitcairn all include guidance on which herbs to administer, how, and in what balance they should be given. Drs. Pitcairn and Schwartz also give information on homeopathic remedies. There is also a wealth of information on the Internet. Use the above resources and, if possible, find a holistic or alternative vet to give you guidance. Not all herbs are advisable for pets so consult a professional to assure a safe vitamin and herb regimen.

The American Holistic Veterinary Medical Association maintains a listing of homeopathic veterinary practitioners in the United States at: *http://www.ahvma.org/states_and_directory/directory.html*

You may also wish to explore alternative therapies, supplementary to your traditional veterinary visits. There are acupuncturists, massage therapists, and chiropractors now training specifically in the treatment of animals. Some holistic or "alternative" vets are actually medically licensed vets who have branched out into holistic care. Holistic care can often offer a more "whole picture" approach to treatment, total body support for general welfare and supportive treatment of chronic conditions and recovery from surgery.

Dr. Schwartz's book gives detailed instructions on how to apply gentle pressure to acupressure points and meridians on your pet to foster general health and promote natural healing. Some holistic practitioners are using magnetic therapies to treat conditions such as arthritis.

Natural Flea Care and Cat Litter

Flea control is a common problem for pet owners and the market does not lack for products that can be applied to your pet externally, given to him orally, and spread around his sleeping area. Many of these commercial products contain some sort of toxin or chemical and come with a warning of how to handle poisoning. Do you really want this to be your animal's flea control?

There is a variety of holistic, natural ways to control fleas. Certain supplements, such as garlic, added to the diet, work very well as natural flea deterrents. Natural baths and flea powders can be made of herbs such as eucalyptus and rosemary, and citronella flea collars can do the work of commercial flea collars without the pesticide residue. Diatomaceous earth, which is really fossilized sea algae remains, can be spread around walls and the base of furniture. Mineral salts are also now being used in some commercial products and by flea treatment companies.

For more information about these products and other natural flea deterrents and remedies, I refer you once again to the books by Dr. Pitcairn and Ms. de Baïracli Levy.

Another area of general welfare for your cat involves the litter tray. Most litter products that sell themselves as odor controlling or clumping litters have additives in them. Add those components to wet paws and you have a potential adverse reaction when your cat ingests the litter when cleaning himself. All felines tend to address their toilette by first licking their paws and then using them to clean the face and body. The use of chemicals to

cloak odors in cat litter is for this reason extremely dangerous in
the long term. A human comparison could be the once common
practice of using scents and sprays to neutralize natural bathroom smells. It seemed like a pretty harmless thing to do until it
emerged that such products were instrumental in the causes of
liver damage. Practically every product or innovation carries
some inherent danger yet the pressure to make use of the latest
modern miracle can be hard to resist. It is often much further
down the road that the full and damaging impact on humans,
animals, and their environment emerges. Pine products can also
cause adverse reactions when ingested. Try to use products that
are all natural, pure clay, or recycled newspaper—they are the
least harmful for your cat and the environment. There are new
litters on the market using milled corn and plant derivatives.
Search the Web for "natural cat litter."

Please don't let all of this information overwhelm you. There
are a number of books and websites to help you educate yourself
on how to shift from conventional, commercialized cat care to a
more natural approach. Take it one day at a time. You and your
cat will be much better for your efforts.

Chapter 9

Miscellaneous Stories

HERE I open my case files and introduce you to some charming felines and their stories, while also offering more information about keeping your cat safe and healthy.

One day Lorraine, who lived in a small cottage in a secluded area, decided she would like to have a cat companion. As she was making breakfast before going to the Society for the Prevention of Cruelty to Animals (SPCA) kennels, she heard a noise. A cat was looking at her through the window, meowing to come in. Lorraine opened the window and the cat jumped into the house, rubbing against her briefly before exploring the cottage, room by room.

At the end of his exploration, he curled up on the couch and went to sleep. Pudlet had found a home and Lorraine had a new cat. Lorraine asked me if Pudlet's arrival was a coincidence. I told her a definite "No."

I have many clients who ask me why all the stray cats in the world arrive on their doorstep. It is because a cat seeking a new home, as Pudlet was, is able to track positive energy vibrations to the place where a cat lover lives. Just as radio waves can be picked up by a receiver tuned to the right frequency, so a cat is able to tune in to the energy vibrations of someone who loves cats or is actively seeking a cat. So Pudlet's arrival was not an accident. He knew before he arrived at Lorraine's house that he would be welcome.

Domestic cats have an ability that has baffled scientists for years. If moved to a new location, they are able to follow an energy link to their old home. Scientists call this PSI-tracking. Cats have found their way home over thousands of miles. Though scientists have a name for it, they don't know how it works or why cats are equipped with such a skill.

Pudlet and Lorraine lived together happily for some years. Then they moved to a new larger house. The move went smoothly but Lorraine and Pudlet were now living in a very different environment, a major adjustment for both of them.

For the first time, Pudlet had his own cat door. He found the new entrance very convenient for going out but didn't realize he could use it to come back inside. Unfortunately, every time Pudlet ventured outside the house, he was attacked by an indignant cat named Calvin who was upset about Pudlet invading his territory.

Lorraine set up a telephone appointment so I could speak

with both cats. As I connected to Pudlet, I was able to tell him he could use the cat door to enter the house. This amused him. He said he would do this and within minutes Lorraine exclaimed, "Sonya, he has just come into the house through the cat door. He's looking very pleased with himself!" Then he turned around and went out only to come back in a few seconds later.

Lorraine loves Pudlet very much. She explained to me how upsetting she found the fighting between the two cats. This had never happened before, as there hadn't been any other cats around their former cottage. Unlike his mum, Pudlet wasn't the least upset by the fighting. In fact, he told me he enjoyed a bit of a scrap.

Calvin, the next-door cat, started talking to me about Pudlet's intrusion. I explained the territory issue to him. He told me he'd already fought for this territory with another cat and it was his. I acknowledged this but explained that Lorraine and Pudlet now lived in this house and garden. I sensed in both cats the feeling they thought they *had* to fight. I explained to both of them that it was okay *not* to fight. That surprised them. I could feel them thinking about it.

Then Pudlet started to tell me things as Calvin listened in to our conversation. Pudlet thought his change of food was disgusting. I told Lorraine what he had said and asked why she had changed the food. She said he was a little on the heavy side. I explained to Pudlet that Lorraine was trying to help him get slim. He said he wanted his old food back. Lorraine agreed to feed him as before but to reduce the portions.

Then Calvin joined in to give his opinion. He agreed Pudlet should have his old food back and asked if Lorraine would give him some too.

Lorraine laughed when Calvin asked me if I were a cat. As usual I told him although I was human, I became a cat when I talked to cats. Both Pudlet and Calvin found this funny and intriguing. Already the two cats' relationship was changing from hostile to friendly, just by talking to me. The thought of good food for Pudlet and some possibility of Lorraine feeding Calvin made them friendlier—almost conspiratorial.

Then Pudlet told me, for some reason, that he liked the brick floor of his new house. Lorraine said she did too. I explained to Pudlet that Lorraine's schedule would take her away from home sometimes. She wanted to know whom he would like to stay with. He said the lady who had looked after him the last time was nice but that Lorraine had a very nice mum who came to the house sometimes and she could look after him too. Lorraine laughed and said she would arrange for one or the other to look after him when she traveled.

I told Lorraine she could talk to Pudlet when she was away. He would hear her. Also, she should always remember to tell him when she was leaving and that she would be back. Lorraine booked another appointment for a month later for me to talk to the two cats again. By then, not only were they getting along, but Calvin had become a lodger. He was using the cat door too, and spending a lot of time with Lorraine and Pudlet. Pudlet was enjoying his new friend's company and both cats were eating good meals served by Lorraine. The disruptive behavior was history.

After eating, the cats often found a patch of sunshine and stretched out together for a nap.

Penny

One day Fitz received a frantic call. Sally, a new client, had a family of four cats, one of which was very sick. The vet couldn't find a cause.

Sally brought me a photograph of all the cats. I tuned in to the vibrations of the sick one, Penny. Immediately I felt my body go weak, so weak I could hardly stand up. Sally told me Penny's symptoms were exactly the same. She kept falling over while trying to stand. I also felt strange vibrations in my nose and a strong smell. Penny said the smell was making her sick. I could feel her nausea. When I asked Sally about this she said they had replaced the carpet a month before and had used smelly adhesives to keep the underlay in place. Penny became sick two weeks after the carpet was fitted.

She was living in a gas chamber full of poisonous gases. Because they are low to the floor where many of these products are used, cats are particularly badly affected by household chemicals. Many are forced to inhale potentially toxic fumes from household sprays, strong-smelling floor cleaners, fly sprays, bleaches and other chemicals commonly used around the house. Some cats become paralyzed from this constant exposure, some even die. As cat lovers, we must be particularly vigilant about the products we use about the house and in the garden. In this case, the other three cats living in the house were not affected by the adhesive smell.

I told Sally to take Penny out of the house as the fumes could kill her. She didn't know if she could stand to be away from Penny now that she was so sick. Unfortunately, it was too late for Penny. Before plans could be made to move her out of the house, she died.

So—I repeat: Please be aware of the products you use in your home. Just because they smell pleasant to you or are purported to kill germs, do not automatically assume they are good for all members of your "family."

The following is a partial list of substances dangerous to cats. Please read labels and become aware of products that can adversely affect your cat.

- Pine cleaning products

- Bleach and products containing bleach

- Any strong-smelling cleaning products

- Strong-smelling paints and adhesives

- Lead, mercury, other heavy metals

- Insect sprays

- Room and fabric deodorizer sprays

- Aspirin and aspirin derivatives

- Tylenol, Motrin, Advil

- Ethylene glycol (found in antifreeze)

- Herbicides and other garden chemicals

- Fertilizers

- Slug pellets

- Creosote

- Household plants such as chrysanthemums, cyclamens, caster bean plants, oleander, dieffenbachia, azalea, caladium, poinsettia (and other Euphorbia), and cherry laurel, among others.

This is only a partial list. Please check all products before using them. If you're unsure, call your vet. Don't just use a product and hope for the best. Select ecology friendly, biodegradable products when possible. Use only dish detergent to wash food and water bowls and rinse them thoroughly with water. If you must use strong cleaners in the home, rinse afterward with vinegar and fresh water to remove dangerous smells and chemicals.

Oliver and Sasha

In this next story, scent is also very important, but this time a little "attitude" adds to the problem.

David and Susan have set up a regular appointment every four months for me to chat with their cats, Oliver and Sasha.

Quite often clients ask me to talk to their cats on a regular basis since they know how important it is to keep their felines informed about vacations, moves or other changes.

Susan and David know they should include their felines in the decision-making process and how this can help prevent problems. In many ways cats are like children, and being sensitive to their feelings and including them in the making of decisions helps them to feel important and loved.

Oliver is an ultrasensitive cat, temperamental and highly strung, with an attitude. Sasha is easygoing, always calm and happy.

When Susan and David first contacted me, it was because Oliver was defecating outside his litter box. They thought the whole situation very strange as Oliver would urinate in the litter box but defecate outside, somewhere close to the box. When I asked Oliver about this, he told me he did not like to use the box after Sasha had used it. He also said the litter smelled bad and hurt his nostrils, so he would urinate inside the box to make it smell better. But the perfume of the litter overpowered his own scent, so he would get outside the box to defecate. The tiles around the box were clean and he was a very clean cat who did not want to use the same box as Sasha.

This differentiation between urinating and defecating may be difficult for some people to understand, but each cat has its own sensitivities and Oliver was particularly sensitive to scents. Susan knew there must be a reason for Oliver's soiling. I told Susan to get another litter box the same color and to buy unscented litter for it. I then told Oliver what was going to happen and thanked him for telling me how he felt. Quite simply, he had hated the smell of the new litter and this is what stopped him defecating in his tray. Susan confirmed that she'd recently been buying a new, perfumed brand.

Oliver immediately also said he liked the scent of his humans around him, thus giving me a very good clue to his problem, so I suggested Susan and David put a little of their urine in his litter box.

They were aghast. I explained that cats love their humans' natural scent. To Oliver this was their urine, the way he could identify them. Having the scent of his humans in his litter box would give him a feeling of comfort and closeness even when they were at work. Their scent in the litter box would encourage Oliver to use it. As I explained about Oliver's sensitivity to scents and how much he liked the smell of his own urine, they accepted that the smell, offensive to them, was pleasing to Oliver and would encourage him to use his new litter box.

I then tuned in to Sasha and asked her if she would please use the litter box she had always used and let Oliver use the new one, otherwise the problem would persist. She said that was fine by her but could she have some new toys and special treats?

I had to laugh. Sasha realized she had an audience and, though she was easygoing, there were no flies on her. She would make the most of the situation by using a bartering technique.

As we know, some cats are quite crafty. Sasha had let it be known that if her human companions wanted her to use the existing litter box, she was happy to oblige, but in return she expected them to reward her. Both David and Susan agreed to her terms. Both cats got new toys and special tuna treats.

Within two days, Oliver was using his new litter box and his behavior was exemplary for over a year. Then came a house move. Just before this I explained to Oliver and Sasha that they were going to relocate and tried to help them understand the situation. I explained the scents of the new house would be different from their old home but they would get used to them. I told them they would be confined to a room for a week so they could form an energy link with their new place, after which they would be let out to explore and discover the rest of the house. I reminded Susan and David how dangerous moving can be for cats and how important it was to provide a safe and secure environment for Oliver and Sasha during all the chaos.

All went well for the first month after the move. Then Oliver began rampaging, waking his human companions every night at 3 A.M. by jumping and running all over the bed. If they shut the door to the bedroom, he scratched and meowed and still woke them. Susan had taken to getting up and going into the lounge with Oliver and sitting with him so David could get some sleep and go to work later. Susan worked from home and was able to sleep a few hours during the day.

I connected telepathically with Oliver and asked him why he was waking his human companions. He told me he was angry with them. They were always busy and his mother was constantly going out during the day and his dad worked and was often away at night. Even when he was home, his dad spent little time with them anymore. Oliver had decided that by waking them at night he could get their attention. Even if they were angry, in his mind it was still attention, and better than no attention at all.

Besides, Oliver continued, they had not given him his toys since the move and, even if he didn't play with them all the time, he liked having them there where he could see them. He did not like the diet he was on and he wanted his old food. He also wanted to know why they had not put the beautiful blue mat under his water bowl. He said it had disappeared since the move and he wanted it back.

I repeated all this to Susan and David. He admitted he had to travel more and Susan said, though she worked from home, she often had to meet clients away from the house. They had been so busy since the move and were often exhausted when they got home.

They still had not unpacked everything, and the box containing the cats' things was still in the garage, unopened. She confirmed she had put Oliver on light food but said she would restore his old diet. I suggested Susan and David spend some quality time each day with their felines. I then asked Oliver not to wake his humans at night and told him the reason. Cats, like children, always want to know why.

I told him that if his human companions did not sleep at night, they would become very tired and unable to work. I then explained why both Susan and David had to work. I said humans have to work to get money to buy food for them and him and to put a roof over everyone's head. He thought about this for a moment, then agreed, but only if his human friends spent time with him during the evening. He insisted that meant they must give him their full attention, not talk to him from the computer when they were busy or speak to him from the kitchen while they were making dinner.

They both laughed and admitted they did often talk to the cats from another room. Oliver and Sasha have completely different personalities. Oliver is insecure by nature while Sasha is quite sure she is loved and did not understand why Oliver was so upset. I explained to Susan and David that Oliver's behavior was typical of a cat with "attitude," and by giving him more attention, the problem would be solved.

The couple made the changes requested, bought him a new blue mat, and gave both cats more attention. Within a few days, Oliver's nocturnal rampages stopped. Oliver again felt special and loved.

Luan

Every client consulting me wants to know how much his or her feline understands of the human world. This case, involving Luan, a Chinese lady whose cats I've worked with quite often, shows just how much cats understand about our human world.

Luan called me quite distressed about the behavior changes in Pebbles and Timothy. Her house had recently been burgled. Since then her cats' behavior had changed completely. They were skittish and frightened all the time and had not ventured out from under the bed. This was unusual as, before the burglary, their behavior had been outgoing and extroverted. They had enjoyed running about the house all day and loved looking out the windows into the garden to watch the wildlife.

Now both cats spent all day and all night huddled together under the bed and refused to come out. They would not even come out to eat.

As I connected to Pebbles, I asked him why he was so nervous. He sent me back a picture of two men breaking a window in his home. Then he told me he and Timothy had run upstairs as fast as they could and hid under the bed. I let him know I understood his nervousness and reassured him it was okay for him to feel this way. It is essential, when speaking to animals, to acknowledge the feelings you receive from them.

Both he and Timothy went on to tell me there had been two men, one very tall and another who was short. Then they sent me a picture of the TV being carried out of the house by the short man. They said their mother was worried the men would come back.

Luan confirmed she was nervous and frightened now. I explained her cats were receiving her fears and emotions. If she could calm down, her two companions would calm down too. Luan told me she had had a burglar alarm fitted in the house the day before and asked could I explain to the cats that if the burglars came back, the noise from the alarm would frighten them away and they would not come into the house. I let the cats know an alarm would begin to ring if burglars returned. This seemed to settle them.

I again reminded Luan the cats could feel her mind energy, feelings, and emotions, transmitted telepathically to her cats.

The calmer she was, the calmer they would be. I could feel Luan relaxing, as she understood she was not helping her cats by being so frightened. I explained the importance of positive thoughts. And reminded her that, with the burglar alarm installed, she should feel safe.

By changing Luan's thoughts and her feelings from insecurity to security, and with the addition of the burglar alarm, the animals soon overcame their fear. Pebbles and Timothy are now their old extroverted selves and enjoy the run of the house.

Boogy

Leslie, a regular client, arrived at my office. I had spoken to her horse often before he passed over. This day she was in tears. She hadn't slept for a week and had been out every night until the early hours, looking for her lovely cat, Boogy.

A guest had left the back door open and her ginger-and-white cat slipped out. As I connected to Boogy, I could feel his anger. He informed me he was very upset with Leslie. I told Leslie, cats will often choose to leave home if they are upset with their human companions.

Boogy went on to tell me his claws had been removed. Leslie tearfully admitted they had. As I have said, claw removal is a grave concern of mine, because I know that without claws, Boogy, or any other cat, is unable to defend himself. Claws are a necessary part of a cat's anatomy. For a lost cat, claws become even more important. Even a domesticated cat, driven by hunger, will try to catch food. For that he needs his claws. I knew time was of the essence. We needed to find Boogy fast.

Boogy began to tell me of his grudges and the reasons he had left home. He had lived happily with his other furry siblings for a number of years until Leslie brought a dog home from the sanctuary without asking Boogy if this was okay with him. It wasn't.

Boogy's list of complaints was long. For a start, he had not been fed top-quality tuna fish in a long time. Canned tuna, sardines, salmon, and mackerel are really hardly any pricier than tinned cat food and much less likely to be pumped full of the revolting waste products and dubious chemicals that we read about earlier. Leslie confirmed he hadn't. He also told me the new dog had disgusting habits and was allowed to eat his food. Also, Leslie had given a party over Christmas with lots of different people and noise and she hadn't even bothered to put Boogy away in her bedroom where he would feel safe. As I told Leslie of his grievances, she was able to see things from Boogy's point of view and began to understand why he had left.

I explained to Boogy how, as human beings, we all make mistakes and asked Leslie to apologize to him, right at that moment, as he could hear her, as well as me, speaking telepathically. I also suggested she tell him she would put everything right for him and in the future, would put him in a different room and feed him away from the dog. I immediately felt Boogy accept Leslie's apology. He lost his anger and calmness came across from him.

I asked Boogy to tell me in which direction he had left. My body felt his body go to the right, down a dip, and then turn left.

He was hiding under a deck. He sent me a picture of a telephone pole and then showed me that he had gone over a fence. He told me he had passed one house with grass and no fence.

I informed him he would have to help himself and listen to me. I could feel his hunger and reminded him Leslie would have tuna waiting at home. (Food is a great motivator.) I told Boogy people were looking for him. Leslie had already posted notices everywhere and put up a reward for his safe return. I told him he should come out and allow people to see him.

As soon as my working day was over, I again connected to Boogy. I felt he was more confident than he had been before. Again I reminded him to keep moving and let humans see him. I felt he was out from under the deck. He was moving around.

Whenever I have a lost animal, I continue to tune in to them, telling them they are not alone, I'm with them. I remind them to keep moving so people can see them. Before I went to bed, I listened to my answering machine. Someone had seen a cat resembling Boogy and Leslie was going to see if it was him.

As it turned out, he was in a yard several blocks away. A couple saw him and called Leslie because they had read her poster. They came right over to Leslie's home and took her to the spot where the cat had been seen. She found Boogy waiting under a bush. He was extremely happy to see her.

Now Leslie puts his dishes up high, away from the dog, gives him lots of tuna and keeps him safe from visitors, so Boogy's happy again.

Jeremiah

One day my husband received a call from a lady in Colorado whose cat had been missing for four months. She had given up all hope of finding him until she heard about me. She had spoken to a number of other animal communicators and had received conflicting reports. One said Jeremiah was dead, another told her he was living in a new home with a family.

Rebecca saw me on a TV program and managed to track down my telephone number through my website. When I spoke with her, I told her I would know if Jeremiah were dead, as he would still come through and speak to me from the other side. I also told her she would have to do her groundwork by putting up posters and asking people in shops, restaurants, and schools to be on the lookout for him.

I explained that I do not always get every cat back through their choosing not to return or because the owner cannot find the target area I describe to them from pictures the cat sends.

As I began looking at a picture of Jeremiah, he began communicating with me, relating details of Rebecca's life only he and certainly not I, could have known. Rebecca was relieved and delighted to learn that her cat was still alive and communicating. Jeremiah told me his journey began after he was taken from his home. I was able to pick up, in great detail, a white car, and then he sent me a picture of a busy airport. Rebecca told me she had taken Jeremiah on a plane journey to Las Vegas to stay with friends.

Jeremiah sent me a picture of the hold of an airplane and the feeling of fear. Then he transmitted another picture of a car, this one grey. Rebecca confirmed her friend had picked them up at the airport in a grey car. The pictures came very fast. Jeremiah flashed me a picture of the interior of Rebecca's friend's home. Jeremiah told me when he was inside the house, the smell was disgusting, meaning, from his point of view, the smell was very different from his own home.

The pictures he was transmitting were quite accurate and Rebecca was amazed as I described each picture to her. I also explained how traumatic this experience had been for Jeremiah, traveling on a plane and staying in a completely different environment. Jeremiah told me that after being in this noisy house with a lot of loud people, his mother let him go outside after only three periods of darkness or three nights. He was pleased to get out of the strange house and away from the loud music.

He started to tell me the direction he had traveled. I sensed he was turning right as he transmitted a feeling with his body to my 'cat' body. At the same time, I was receiving landmarks. I did not feel any hunger or thirst in Jeremiah's body, so I knew he was being fed and had access to water.

Next he sent me a picture of a large building with lots of cars and lights and told me the cars moved a lot. The building had a red roof and, at the same time as that picture, Jeremiah sent me the smell of food. I estimated he'd traveled about two miles. He told me he was living with many other cats. I told Rebecca he was not living with people. He informed me he was an outdoor cat and transmitted images of the back of the building with large dustbins and men wearing navy blue striped outfits bringing food to feed him and the other cats.

Rebecca was amazed. She knew the location. It was a casino. By the time I finished the consultation, Rebecca was happy. I suggested she telephone the casino in Las Vegas to ask who fed the cats. She said she would fly to Las Vegas from Colorado to continue the search.

I warned her to plan to stay at least a week, as, after a cat has adapted to a completely different lifestyle, his behavior could be quite different. After living wild, he could revert back to instinctual behavior and I warned her not to be disappointed if, just by calling his name, he didn't come immediately, I suggested she wait in the casino parking lot and observe quietly from her car. I asked her to call me when she arrived in Las Vegas.

A few days later, Rebecca called. She had spoken to the casino and sent them a picture of Jeremiah. The chef was feeding many cats and one resembled her Jeremiah. Rebecca's flight was booked for the following morning, and she promised to keep me informed when she arrived in Las Vegas. The next day there was an excited message. She had seen Jeremiah in the parking lot at the casino but a car had driven in and he had run away. She had also talked to the chef who fed all the cats and asked him if he could help her catch Jeremiah.

The next morning I called Rebecca. She was overjoyed and told me she had her cat back. The chef had managed to grab Jeremiah as he was eating.

Nonetheless she was quite concerned because he was frightened and not responding to her at all. I reminded her he had been living wild for four months and to give him time to adjust. I also suggested when she arrived home, not to let him out for at least three weeks. I emphasized to Rebecca how important a regular routine was for Jeremiah. During the time he had lived outside, he had reverted to living by his instincts. This self-reliance can produce problems in some cats since an independent cat sees little benefit in cooperating with humans.

Rebecca needed to understand it was going to take patience on her part for Jeremiah to settle back and only time would tell if he wanted to be a house cat again. A few months passed before Rebecca contacted me again to say Jeremiah had again gone missing and not returned. As I tuned in to Jeremiah, he informed me he no longer wanted to live as a house cat and he would not be coming back. He had his territory and had found a lady who fed him outside.

Though Rebecca was upset about him leaving, she knew he no longer wanted to live indoors. She also knew he had not forgiven her for taking him on a plane to a strange place. From time to time, Rebecca books some time with me so she can find out how Jeremiah is doing. Jeremiah always informs me he is happy living the natural life of a feral cat. He is independent and prefers to live his life this way. Jeremiah no longer felt he could rely on Rebecca as she lived a stressful life and had moved many times, so he decided to change to a life where he could take care of himself. He is now happy, living his way.

Judy

Judy is the fourteen-year-old feline companion of my friend Valerie Patrick. Judy and Val also share their home with two dogs: a golden retriever and an Alsatian. All the animals live harmoniously. Judy, who is a very independent cat and can be a little sullen, has always been used to living with dogs. If one of the dogs irritated her, she would smack it hard with her claws out and the dog would beat a retreat. All Judy wanted was a little respect. She expects them to understand that she's in charge.

One day Val's son Edwin came to visit. He brought his dog, a boxer named Duke that he had rescued from the humane society. Since Val understands dogs can be territorial, Duke and her two dogs were introduced outside the house and taken for a walk together, then brought back into the garden. As they were released from their leads, Duke spotted Judy in the garden and ran with great speed toward her, barking.

Val had not known Judy was stretched out in the sun. Judy was very frightened by this intruder in her usually safe garden and fled over the fence. Judy usually sleeps in the sun or investigates the garden during the day, but she always waits by the door to come into the house at night. She rarely ventures out of her garden.

But that evening Judy was nowhere to be seen. Val called me, very distressed, the next day. She had been up all night calling and looking but to no avail. I explained to Val that when cats are afraid, they will hide and stay hidden until it feels it is safe to come home. Even if it hears you calling, the cat will lie low until its instincts say it's safe to come out. This can sometimes take two or three days, depending on the personality of the cat.

As I tuned in to Judy, I could feel her fear. I told her that Duke had left that morning. She replied she was well aware of this but was not ready to come out yet. I told her Val was terribly upset. She had not known Edwin was bringing Duke with him. If she had realized, she would have made sure Judy was in the house and safe. I asked Judy to come home. She said she was close to the house. I emphasized how her absence was upsetting Val and asked if she could tell me where she was. She sent me a picture of a fence and some shrubbery. At the same time, I could feel my "cat" body pressed up against the fence.

Val has a large garden. I told her to look in the shrubbery near the fence on the left of the garden. The next day Val's message said she still hadn't found Judy. The night before, Val had camped outside with a flashlight, calling Judy over and over, during the night, but she had not appeared. That day Ruby, Val's housekeeper, arrived. Ruby loves Judy and immediately set out to search the garden again. She found Judy, close to the fence, in the left-hand corner of the garden.

If you have a cat and you know friends are arriving with their dog, be sure to explain the situation to the cat and confine him to a room where he will feel safe. It is a great comfort to a cat when their human companions take the time to tell them what's happening.

Dogs love to chase cats and many cats will simply disappear until the unwanted guest is gone. Unlike dogs, cats do not always come when called. If they are afraid, they will freeze in a protected place until their instincts tell them it is safe to come out. That can take a week. Meanwhile, the human companion will continue to be worried and distraught, as Val was.

Fortunately, I was able to talk to Judy, discover she was still in the garden, and get a direction in which she had run so Ruby was able to find her and bring her back inside the house.

Because cats have such diverse personalities and are able to make decisions about their own welfare, they are endlessly fascinating creatures. But they have another remarkable skill that we will examine in more detail soon. Cats are psychic and are able to see into the spiritual realm. So next, I will share with you some wonderful stories about psychic felines and their startling abilities.

Chapter Ten

Cats Leaving Only to Return

I DO not ever doubt that we have lived many times before and experienced many lifetimes on this physical plane and that there is a link from our material world to the spiritual one.

I can and do interact both with people and animals on the other side. I know that when many of my clients are grieving, they have found peace through knowing their animals are still close to them and that, when an animal dies, there is no separation. Only the physical body dies. Time and time again, when an animal has passed over to the spirit world, it will come back to make contact with its loved ones on earth.

My spiritual guides tell me that animals are divine souls and have the choice of coming back to the physical plane to learn, just as humans do. They also tell me that when our time comes to journey on to the spiritual dimension, the loved ones and animals we have shared our lives with are there, waiting to greet us.

Frequently, when a client has a consultation with me to talk to their feline or other animal, a departed human loved one will come through holding a feline that has passed over. Or a dog will walk in with them when I open the door to greet them and, following close at their heels, will sit down beside them. Many of us share our lives with animals, unaware that the animals are here to teach us—sometimes about love. Contrary to some people's beliefs, animals do have souls. Some are divine spiritual angels.

When I hear of animals being abused, it makes me sad and angry. There is never an excuse for this sin. Animals have so much love to give us. Often they are even able to teach us to forgive, as they are extremely forgiving. Many clients feel anguish and guilt when a furry companion passes over. Perhaps they feel they didn't get the medications right or they left the animal in pain too long before they put it to sleep. I am often asked to apologize for them. The animal that has transcended into the spiritual world always tells me there is nothing to forgive.

If you do the best you can for the animal, don't attack yourself by having feelings of guilt or feeling you have failed it. Your feline friend does not see the situation as you do.

You and he still have a spiritual connection. By talking to him, knowing and feeling he is still with you, there is no separation. You cannot see the physical body, but his energy is still with you and energy cannot be destroyed. No cat can ever take the place of a cat that has passed on, but death is a natural part of life. Cats do not share many humans' fear of death. They have the ability to see into another dimension as well as the capability of seeing spirits.

How many times have you seen a cat dashing across a room, chasing something unseen . . . unseen to humans, that is, but not to the cat? Cats are psychic. From my experiences I believe all animals are spiritual and communicate on a higher level of consciousness than humans. They have no fear of death because they know they will be traveling to a place of joy and peace when they leave their physical form. So when their time comes to leave, give them your blessing and let them go. Tell them it is all right for them to go. They understand you are feeling deep sadness and they often don't want to leave the family, even though their bodies have aged and they are ready to leave.

The feline knows he is going to travel on to a wonderful dimension and is looking forward to leaving his often pain-wracked body. He knows his journey will take him where he will reunite with loved ones, both animal and human. Those waiting on the other side will greet your beloved pet with love and joy as he leaves his physical body to return to the spiritual realm.

Just as we buy a new car when the old one wears out, so our physical body is a vehicle for us to travel in until it breaks down and wears out. The time comes for all beings to leave their bodies and go on. We do not go into a void or nothingness. We go to a beautiful dimension where we are greeted with joy and love.

Cats have extensions of all the senses humans have lost or are not using. They have a subtle, silent language that they transmit through the universal energy fields. They are wise and clairvoyant. They have the ability to reach levels of consciousness most humans are unable to reach or understand. Cats understand that death is to be celebrated or rather that there is no death. A cat knows he can still travel to the next dimension and can choose to come back in another physical form.

We humans can also choose to return but, unlike the human, the cat will sometimes know this before he leaves this dimension. Some cats tell me to inform their owners that they will be returning to them in another physical form. The cat understands he is much more than a physical body during his physical life. He is born with the knowledge that he can reach far beyond his physical form. He may return as a cat or another animal—never as a human.

Though you can no longer hold your pet and stroke his fur or hear his meow, the wise cat can still visit you in his spiritual form. When a cat leaves his physical body, his energy is still felt and some humans can feel this. You must be open to this experience and allow yourself to feel his presence by sensing his energy. If you experience this feeling, trust your intuition and know your cat is visiting you in energy form.

My client Jan, whose cat passed over, experiences the energy of her cat Milo lying on her pillow near her hair, and can feel him as she did when he was in his physical form. Jan has lovely long hair that Milo loved to sleep on. She can still sometimes feel Milo's energy on her pillow as she drops off to sleep. It's a great comfort to her as she knows he is visiting her and sleeping, as he always did, curled up on her hair.

Jan uses her intuitive senses to feel his presence and talks to him as they both share these moments that Jan calls "Milo and Jan's pillow talk." She has seen him flash across the room and she knows he has not left her as her heart jumps for joy each time she enjoys this incredible spiritual experience.

My wonderful cat Wellington passed away at twenty-one years of age. How lucky we were to have his physical form with us for so long. Just before he left us, he told me he would be coming back very soon. Within five months Wellington was reincarnated back into our lives. His beautiful new body is, at the time of writing this book, one year old. I'd like to share Wellington's story with you.

From a Goose to a Cat, Part One

As I explained when I began this book, one of the few tragedies of my childhood was the death of my three beloved geese, Primrose, Buttercup, and Daisy. When their lives were cut short, I stopped communicating with animals in that special way I had all through my childhood.

From the day my three great friends were born, they responded to my love and kindness and I to theirs. We were a family and we shared wonderful experiences. I would sit in the fields and chat with them for hours. They commiserated with me about my family problems and I listened to their intrigues.

Primrose was the first one to peck her way out of her shell and I was present when she performed this miracle. From the day she was born, she was always rather bossy and determined.

The geese helped me with my work. I worked for my father in his shop and had a morning paper route. This was fun since my dog Silky, Buttercup, Primrose, and Daisy plus a number of the other village animals joined me as we walked through the lanes and fields delivering the newspapers to each cottage.

All the other animals living with human companions greeted us, and the cows that grazed on the grass in the local farmer's field would walk with us until I laid the farmer's paper on the kitchen table of his three-hundred-year-old farmhouse. I would often wake up the villagers as I let myself into their cottages with the key on a piece of string behind the letterbox. I would call up the stairs to them and put the kettle on for the early morning cup of tea, leave their paper, then continue on my round.

Mr. Skeers, whose paper I delivered, lived with his cat companion, Tom. Mr. Skeers was a kindhearted old gentleman and loved Tom dearly. Mr. Skeers always slept downstairs on a bed in front of the coal fire. The bedroom proper was too cold for him in winter as there was no fireplace upstairs. He slept in all the clothes he wore during the day and bathed twice a year, at least that's what my friend Aunt Rene told me. She's the one who worked for my father in the shop but would also clean Mr. Skeers's cottage for him every so often. Old Mr. Skeers said he did not do woman's work like dusting and sweeping.

Tom slept with him and greeted me each morning as my menagerie and I came into the cottage. There was no running water and on my way in I would fill up the kettle from the tap outside, then I would give Tom his usual saucer of milk. Primrose loved Tom and they were good friends. Tom would snuggle up to Primrose very affectionately and Primrose would be embarrassed. She informed me she would have liked to be a cat so she could sleep on my bed each night like Mr. Skeers's cat slept with him.

This happy relationship with my geese continued for nine months. I spent idyllic days in their company until the Christmas of 1950. That Christmas was the only sad one of my childhood, as I have said. Father killed my three geese for food, doing what was routine for him. Raising stock for food was his way of life.

After the heartbreak I suffered when my three geese were killed, it would be many years before I began talking to the animals again.

For all of us who share our lives with animals, the time comes when we must say goodbye to their physical form, and their spirit journeys on to their home in the spiritual realm. Some of us are very fortunate when we find an animal's spirit has returned to us in a new physical body. Animals choose, sometimes, to reincarnate to the earth plane, just as humans do, and then, if we are extremely fortunate, we can again share a new loving lifetime with that dear soul again.

From a Goose to a Cat, Part Two

Wellington was born a farm cat in a beautiful part of the English countryside, the village of Downe in Kent where Charles Darwin was born. He was a bundle of black fur with deep amber eyes. He used to chase after our two Rhodesian Ridgeback dogs and play with them. He was fearless and became bonded to Boru, the male Ridgeback, hanging on to the loose skin under Boru's chin while Boru walked around.

From the time he came into my life, I felt we had been together before. For some years after Fitz and I married we lived in London and thoroughly enjoyed the variety and pace of city life. But at heart I was still a country girl and when we had the chance of acquiring a cottage near Farnborough in Kent, we grabbed it and moved. Our flint cottage was an eighteenth-century Grade II listed building, nestling in woodland and farmland, next to a golf course, close to the Downs yet easy for transport to London, and quite near Gatwick Airport. It suited us so well.

Each night Wellington would sleep curled up on my bed. I rose early every morning to take a long walk with the dogs across the golf course and into the woods. One morning when Wellington was about six months old, I had walked for about two miles in the woods when I saw Boru and his friend Bella being ambushed. Something, moving very quickly, jumped out at them, then disappeared back into the bushes. Both dogs began barking. As I went toward them, out of the bushes came Wellington. He meowed and came strutting toward me along the grassy wooded pathway with a self-assured swagger.

High in the sky, the morning sun glistened through the trees and a white spiritual glow surrounded his black physical form. Then the picture began to change and I saw, in my mind's eye, a flashback to one of my geese, Primrose. At the same time, I experienced a nostalgic feeling. It became clear that I was about to share another lifetime, some thirty years later, with my reincarnated goose friend Primrose. This time she had chosen to return in the physical body she had wanted to be in.

In the blink of an eye, I remembered her communicating to me, "I would like to be able to sleep on your bed each night just like Mr. Skeers's cat."

The premonition I was experiencing was one of only five I have experienced in my lifetime.

From that day on, each time I walked the dogs, Wellington would follow behind, hiding in the bushes. Then he would ambush the dogs. I somehow understood that this special beautiful spirit, Wellington, had chosen to come back to my life.

When he reincarnated from a short life as a goose, he lived in his reincarnated cat body for twenty-one years. Not only was I lucky in Primnose coming back as a cat, she also brought back and rekindled my ability to talk to the animals. It had been the pain of her leaving before that had shut the door to my talking to animals all those years ago. Wellington reopened that door in his second lifetime with me and gave me the gift back.

Rosie's Surprise: Wellington Returns Again

In chapter four, you read how Rosie came to us. Now her story continues: Rosie settled into our home quickly. It was extraordinary how she accepted all the dogs and had no fear of them whatsoever. If they came too close to her, she would box them with her paws and they would hastily retreat. The dogs treated her with friendly affection and respect. Just days after her arrival, I noticed Rosie's shape was changing. One side of her body was protruding as though she was expecting kittens.

We visited the vet, who gave her a thorough examination and confirmed she was about six weeks pregnant and still very undernourished. With us to take care of her, Rosie no longer needed to worry about starvation and she no longer needed to fend for herself. As time passed, Rosie began to tell me about her past life; about how she was so hungry she went inside the humans' houses hoping someone would feed her. About how a man in a trailer would kick her. She hurt all over from the impact of his large boot on her frail frame. She landed on the ground and hurt even more. After that, she was afraid to go inside the trailer when he was there.

Then sadness emanated from her as she began to tell me about her mother. First the love came as she remembered the smell of her mother and how her mother protected and loved her, how they played together and her mother's gentleness. Her mother hunted for food for them both and they lived under the trailer. There was rubbish there where they could hide. She loved the warmth of her mother's body when they curled up close together.

Then one day her mother went to hunt for food and did not return. When darkness came, Rosie ventured out to search and found her mother and thought she had fallen asleep, but she couldn't get her to move. She had been hit and killed by a car.

Rosie became terribly sad. I asked her to continue her story and told her that one day she would meet her mother again in a beautiful place where she would be happy. She informed me that she knew, as she could see her mother in the spiritual realm, but she still missed her very much.

She continued her story, which I have put into my words.

For some time she tried to make her mother get up, but she didn't move. Rosie became fearful, then, as two dogs came running toward her. She ran up a tree to get away from them and stayed there for the rest of the night. After her mother's death, she had very little food and was terribly hungry. Some days a little girl brought her food and tried to play with her.

Then one night a beautiful black spirit cat came to her and told her to follow him. He said he lived in the spirit world and was in the same dimension as her mother. He told her he did special work and he was going to help her. I instinctively knew the black cat she mentioned was my cat Wellington who had passed away only a few months before.

Rosie followed the spirit cat until he stopped in the darkness and told her to wait, a white van would be coming up the drive and a man would be in the van, a kind man that could help her, but she must let him see her. The spirit cat said he would wait with her. Rosie told me she felt safe with the black cat and he stayed with her until she saw the van lights beaming.

The van driver was my husband, Fitz. Wellington had led Rosie to Fitz, knowing Fitz would help this beautiful tabby.

I now knew that one day Wellington would return to us. At our house, Rosie dined on fresh fish, turkey and chicken cat food served to her on beautiful china saucers on her own personal placemat. She devoured all the food that was placed in front of her. As the days passed and Rosie's time drew near, I moved her to her own "apartment" so she could be away from the excitement and noise of the other animals. I felt a quieter environment was better for a pregnant feline. I was on the phone talking to my friend Sylvia's two dogs, Topaz and Brandy, when I saw Rosie going into labor. Her contractions began about half past five in the afternoon. I asked Sylvia to hold on while I covered my sofa with towels and sheets. Then, as I continued to talk to Sylvia, Rosie jumped up by my side. Within five minutes she was beginning to bear down.

By this time, Sylvia was as excited as I was. Though I'm not a drinker, I was so carried along by Sylvia's enthusiasm that I could have downed a large whisky just to steady my nerves. I found I was quite anxious. I asked Dr. Thompson, my spirit guide, to help me. He told me Rosie was capable of taking care of everything. How right he was, but she did have a difficult labor with each of the three kittens.

Rosie let out a scream as the first kitten arrived, then began purring and washing him. The impact of this new arrival was stunning. As I watched Rosie clean the new kitten's long tabby-marked body and saw his lovely face with his eyes tight shut, I knew that Wellington had returned.

Golden Boy

My friend Claire called to ask how her eighteen-year-old cat Golden Boy was feeling. Claire is a great animal lover and, like me, opens her home to many unwanted and neglected animals.

Golden Boy had arrived on her doorstep and Claire and her daughter Judy who were already living with eight cats and seven dogs, as well as feeding some feral cats, took him in. Both of these ladies have great love and compassion for animals and listen to their hearts, not their heads. Both know that one of the main needs of all animals, feral or domesticated, is a roof over their heads.

The feral cats have a large dog kennel to shelter in when winter comes. The other animals live in the house. All the animals have been spayed and neutered, an essential part of helping to control the animal population and spare more animals from being homeless.

When Claire called me this time, Golden Boy had shared twelve years with her and Judy but now his physical form was wearing out. He could not always get to the litter box in time. His bladder and bowels weren't functioning efficiently. This distressed him, as he had always been clean and quite particular about using the litter box or the garden.

Claire is in touch with her animals and can talk to them telepathically. Ironically, when we are specially close to an animal that becomes sick, it is often difficult to communicate with it, as our own emotional body is a wreck. Our human feelings play a large part when communicating with animals and, when we're distressed or overly emotional, it's difficult to communicate effectively with our animals.

As a beloved animal approaches death, it is distressing, even though death is a part of life. Claire understood there would be no separation when Golden Boy left his physical form, as energy cannot die. But the thought of not sharing a physical form together, of letting go, was difficult. Golden Boy told me he was ready to leave. Claire had instinctively known this and just wanted confirmation. She had made the decision by trusting what her heart and intuitions were telling her. Claire and Judy had already given permission for Golden Boy to go on to the spiritual realm, and she was hoping that he would leave his body without the help of a vet.

Though the decision is painful, you will help your cat so much if you can find the courage to tell him it's okay to go, as many cats will try to stay longer to please us humans. This is selfish on our part because, when they leave, they are leaving their pain behind. Your cat is journeying to a wonderful place where he will no longer suffer.

Without question one of the most difficult decisions that animal lovers face is that of letting go. Time and time again clients consult me, seeking counsel on the awesome responsibility of playing God with one of their beloved pets and it is not unusual for this decision to be made and remade on a number of occasions. The situation can create real anguish.

Claire and Judy made the decision to take Golden Boy to the vet's office. Judy drove with Golden Boy lying on a blanket on Claire's knee. As they pulled to a stop in front of the vet's office Golden Boy left his physical body. All of his animal friends from the spiritual realm were happily awaiting his return. Golden Boy had no more pain.

Golden Boy knew that his spiritual form would always be with Claire and Judy, and although they miss his physical form, they sense and feel his energy all around them.

$\mathcal{L}$eonardo

Marcia has five cats, one dog, and a bird. Marcia and I work very closely together as she is responsible for organizing my animal communicating seminars and workshops and is always accompanied everywhere by her faithful companion, Margaux, a Tibetan terrier.

When I have a TV appearance, Margaux often appears on the show, and when TV producers and film crews come to my home to film my thirteen animals, Margaux is always filmed along with them. When Marcia is working in my office, Margaux is with her "helping." Though small, Margaux takes her work seriously. If my dogs make too much noise, Margaux intervenes and tells them to be quiet. They always back off as they have respect for her.

When she's at home, Margaux takes care of her five cat companions. Some years ago, there had been a very special cat in Margaux's life, Leonardo. Margaux and Leonardo were inseparable. He slept with Margaux and she would even allow him to eat from her food bowl whereas if the other cats tried that she would run them off. The two animals shared a close friendship until June of 1996 when, at the age of fourteen, Leonardo died from a kidney infection and passed over to the spirit world. Both Marcia and Margaux were sad for a long while.

In 1998, Marcia was visiting her mother in St. Louis when Margaux became ill with a bladder infection. Marcia rushed her to a vet. As they were waiting, Margaux started to whine and pull forward on her leash. When Marcia looked across the room to see what had drawn her attention, she saw a cage with a small kitten in it. Above the cage was a sign reading PET ADOPTION. Both Marcia and Margaux were captivated with the small creature in the cage and fell instantly in love with him.

Now Marcia had not only one furry companion occupying her on her journey back home to Houston, but two! When they got into her car at the airport in Houston, Marcia placed the crate with the kitten on the back seat and opened the front door for Margaux who always travels sitting in the front seat next to her. For the very first time, Margaux insisted she sit in the back seat with the kitten. Each time Marcia called her to come and sit in the front, Margaux stayed put, and would not leave the kitten's side. Marcia found her behavior quite unusual because Margaux had always liked sitting in the front seat.

When Marcia pulled into her drive, she decided to take the animals in through the front door. Normally she would drive around to the back into the garage and use the back door. As she entered her hall, she placed the crate with the kitten on the floor and opened the door to allow Hennessey, as the kitten had been named, out. Without any hesitation, Hennessey walked out. Marcia noticed Hennessey leaned to the right when he walked, just as Leonardo had.

But more amazingly, Hennessey walked straight through the kitchen into the laundry room and used the blue litter box that Leonardo had always used. Then the new arrival went to the cabinet where the feeding bowls and food were kept and opened the door with his little paws, just like Leonardo.

Just then Champion, an old cat who had played with Leonardo, came running through the kitchen at great speed to greet Hennessey. They rubbed up against each other with obvious pleasure. It was then than Marcia knew for sure—Leonardo had returned to them. No doubt Margaux wondered why she had taken so long, since she had recognized Leonardo's spirit instantly.

Occasionally an animal will decide to change its form when it returns to the earth plane. The next story is about just such a change.

Samuel Returns

Keith and Francis are two friends who live in Northamptonshire. When I first knew them, they were sharing their lives with two cats, Belinda and Spike, and a dog named Samuel, their faithful companion of thirteen years. Samuel had been an only pet for eight years before the arrival of the cats. Yet he helped look after them as kittens and was gentle and kind to both when they became adults.

All three animals shared their food dishes and bed.

After six years of living with his feline friends, it was time for Samuel to leave his physical body. All of Samuel's family was devastated. As we all know, the pain is over for our furry companion, but each time we have to say goodbye to the physical form of our animal friends, we feel intense sadness and then we have to learn to live without them.

Keith decided not to adopt another dog as Spike and Belinda had had such a wonderful loving relationship with Samuel, they felt no dog could fulfill their expectations. They were happy with their cats and wanted everything to stay that way. Three years slipped by without any other animals being added to the household. Only the passing of time can make a difference to the way we feel about losing a pet. But when the time is right, and sometimes in an unexpected way, an animal can come into our lives.

Keith and Francis are both chefs. One day as Keith left the hotel where he worked, he saw a small, very thin tabby cat. He went back to the kitchen, cut up some chicken and took it, on a paper plate, to the cat. The cat came to him immediately, meowing and purring, and began to eat. The next day when Keith arrived for work, he was greeted in the car park by the cat meowing and rubbing his head against his leg. Keith picked the tabby up as the weather was cold and frost covered the ground.

He decided to leave the cat in the bar where Francis worked so he could keep an eye on him. Snow had been forecast for the night and the little cat had nowhere to go and no shelter. It curled up beside the open log fire in the bar and stayed there all day. That night Keith and Francis decided to take him home to see how Belinda and Spike would feel about him. They finished work around midnight and drove home, apprehensive at introducing the kitten to the others.

When they put the small cat down in the house, they couldn't believe what they saw. The little cat ran toward Spike and Belinda, who greeted him with affection. Then they began checking him out all over, even sniffing down his legs to his paws. The small cat rubbed up against them both, meowing softly, then walked into the kitchen and went on to examine each room of the cottage with Belinda and Spike running after him. Keith and Francis were amazed. It was as if the cats had known each other for years. Over the next few days, the little cat, now called Basil, made himself at home.

One of the endearing things old Samuel had done, was to nibble Keith's ear to wake him. He would push his nose up to Keith's ear every morning and gently rouse him. This was just one of the many things Keith missed after Samuel passed over. Now Basil took over the job of waking Keith in the morning. He would jump on his bed and walk all over him. One morning, Keith, who had drunk a little too much whisky the night before and had a hangover, didn't get up when Basil walked over him.

After a time, Basil began walking over his head. Then Keith felt his ear lobe being gently chewed. Hangover or no, Keith awakened joyfully, full of gratitude for what he was experiencing. He had absolutely no doubts—Samuel had returned to him in a new physical form.

Sanctuary

While cats do not share the human fear of death, they still experience the pangs of grief in the case of either the departure of a human or a companion animal. In some instances they will refuse to eat, since the intensity of their grief takes their appetite away. Cats can become devoted to another cat or animal living with them. They are capable of feeling deep love for each other. When the physical form is no longer there and although they can see the spiritual form of their companion in the spiritual realm, they miss the physical form. There have been instances where they will grieve and die, knowing this way they can be together in the spiritual realm.

Here is a sad, touching example of the resolve and dedication of cats when they confront the death of a loved human companion. Special Pals Animal Sanctuary near Houston, Texas, contacted me. Special Pals have a "no kill" policy and provide homes for cats and dogs, as well as potbellied pigs and other species of animals that need rescuing.

The Sanctuary had taken in four cats whose human companion had died. They hoped that after a period of recovery and adjustment in the specially designed cat house at the Sanctuary, where the animals receive not only boundless love but also the very best veterinarian care, the cats would enter their adoption program. Although the cats were apparently in good health when they arrived, they were, as are all new arrivals, given a thorough physical examination. All seemed fine except one had a nonthreatening liver problem. But it soon became apparent that all was not well. Soon their conditions began to deteriorate. By the time the Sanctuary contacted me, two of them had died.

I established communications both with the two cats who were left in their physical bodies and the two who were reunited with their owner in the spiritual plane. The two cats still in their physical bodies could see their owner's energy body and their grief was so painful, all they wanted to do was get out of their physical form so they could be with her. They had no desire to stay in this dimension now that she had left.

Cats know what they want. They are extremely independent, more independent than any other species on the planet. These felines wanted to join their departed human companion. The two cats who had died had already made that choice and left. As I spoke to the third cat, who was extremely emaciated and very weak, he was adamant in his resolve to die and follow his companions. Knowing that he had made up his mind, I contacted Carol at the Sanctuary. She was considering force-feeding this cat to help him regain strength. I told her that, in my opinion, it would be better to accept the inevitable and let him go. Carol admitted she'd already been thinking along the same lines.

The fourth cat had a different personality. I was able to convince him he still had work to do in this dimension. I communicated to him that he could bring great happiness to another human companion and he could experience love and happiness himself. I discovered he was not quite as determined to go as his friends. He still had the will to live.

After I explained to him how the Sanctuary would find him a really happy home, he was intrigued and interested in what I had to say. Subsequently, he appeared with the Sanctuary Director Salise Shuttlesworth on a TV program and to my delight the Sanctuary found him a very happy home.

The two cats who had died and been reunited with their owner had achieved their purpose and were happy. They looked forward to the arrival of the third cat. All three cats and their owner accepted that the fourth cat had work to do on the earth plane but that one day he would be reunited in the spiritual realm with his friends, once again.

Many of us have experienced the loss of a cat. No one can take from you the love, joy, and wonderful memories of the time you spent together, and one day, when your time comes to journey to the spiritual realm, you will be reunited.

Epilogue

THROUGHOUT my life, I have helped and rescued many animals and I continue to do so. Many of them have been cats. Sadly, there are a great number of unwanted cats that find themselves in shelters because of overpopulation and human neglect.

Cats taken to animal shelters know instinctively if they are to be put to death. The time leading up to euthanasia is traumatic to a healthy cat as most do not want to die and somehow sense the horrifying prospect before the shameful act is committed. Overall, the United Kingdom is making progress in the necessity of emphasizing and promoting a social conscience that calls for changes in attitude and feline welfare to reduce the size of this problem.

The problem is even more acute in the United

States, but here again changing attitudes and the pioneering work of the growing number of no-kill shelters is forcing the pace for more humane treatment. Many good-hearted people all over the world feed wild and feral cats. This is important. But to my mind, the most valuable thing we can do for the cats that come into our care, be they wild or domestic, is to have them neutered.

Simply feeding cats, especially feral cats, without having them neutered is irresponsible. Better nutrition leads to more unwanted kittens that are faced with starvation and disease. Neutering makes a huge difference to the quality of a feral cat's life, especially females, who can die a terrible death giving birth in the wild.

Once they've been neutered, by all means, return the cat to the wild if they are feral. Though some rescued feral cats settle into homes, many hate losing their freedom and prefer returning to the wild world they know. But do, please, continue feeding them. Providing food, neutering, and veterinary care for a large number of cats can become costly. If money is an issue, find a way of raising it or working with local vets. There are many devoted cat lovers who are willing to help. Even a small group of people having garage sales or asking for donations can raise enough money to help a great number of cats. Don't be afraid to ask people for money. I find most animal lovers are only too willing to help.

Many people have seen my ability to talk to animals on television shows in both the United Kingdom and the United States and have heard of my work through profiles on national news programs. I always try to bring abused and neglected animals on to the show in an attempt to raise awareness of their plight as well as to find homes for these neglected animals.

People are constantly astonished at what animals tell me both on camera and off. I have been instrumental in raising people's consciousness about animals' intelligence. Humans need to understand that animals have language, they have feelings and emotions, and they can feel happiness and some even cry when they're sad. Animals are as aware of their surroundings as you or I, and they deserve to be treated with kindness and respect.

Cats are very special, independent spirits. Each has well-developed intuition and awareness. They are mystical and instinctively know how to use the natural elements of the universe. They have the ability to see beyond the physical world and are wonderful teachers if we choose to learn from them.

I hope this book has helped you in your relationship with your cat. I entreat you to care responsibly for every cat that comes into your life. Don't even consider having them declawed.

If you see lost or abandoned animals, don't pass them by. Go out of your way to help those animals, perhaps even take them into your home. If you are unable to keep the animals, try to find them good homes. Don't support organizations that profit from animal exploitation. Don't buy products from manufacturers who test their products on animals.

Please join me in my fight to reduce the suffering of animals and make their world a better place.

Please help.

Thank you.

Some Faxes, Letters, and Emails I've Received

AUGUST 8, 1998

Sonya,

Please find the detail of the reading as follows.

Pele ran away a week after my family returned from their holiday in Majorca. You correctly read that the main reason to her running away was she was unhappy at being put into a cattery. She had also been ill and refusing to eat. Pele communicated to you that the plates had been changed the day she ran away from "people's plates" to "cat" dishes—you actually advised me of this before I asked my parents, who confirmed this to be the case.

You also correctly communicated with Pele who told you that she slept on my sister's (Lois) bed, which was covered with lots of cushions, that my sister sings a lot, that Pele loves to have the stereo on and that her favorite toy had recently been put away. Another point was that Pele was worried about my mum (Diane) limping (which was due to her suffering from polio as a child) and you reassured her that Mum is all right and not suffering.

To try and persuade Pele to come back, you told us to put out her favorite food—tuna—give her back her original dishes and she should return as darkness falls.

And—according to plan—this happened!!

Take care and I look forward to speaking to you soon.

Lots of love,

Naomi

FAX

SUBJECT: I HEALED A PURPLE MARTIN TODAY!!!!!!!!!!!!!!!!

DATE: 10/9/00 5:37 P.M.

FROM: MARIE

Dearest Sonya and Denis,

WOWWIE!!!!!! You all wouldn't believe what happened this afternoon! A purple martin slammed into our living-room window. I went outside and found the poor baby all sprawled out on the ground in a puddle of water. So I picked him up and took him in the garage where it was warm and dry. Then I sat with him and prayed to God, Dr. Thompson, Edgar Casey, St. Francis, the bird's angels, and my angels to help me heal him. Soon, white light flowed through his whole body, then purple, then pink, and then blue. He was so relaxed he had his eyes closed. I kept at it until nothing else came to me. Then I took him outside and he flew off!!!!! I had never tried to heal a wild animal before! Oh Sonya, thank you so much for teaching me how to heal! You are an angel here on earth!!!! And congratulations on your TV appearance on A&E's "The Unexplained"!!!! You were wonderful and beautiful!!! I recorded it. Rusty is doing really well but would love to see you again!! As would all of us!!!

    Your Friends,

    Marie, James, Rusty, Ernie, Xena, Casey, Shadow, Jax, and Michaela Vlasin.

CARD FROM PHYLLIS AND DIXIE:

Dear Sonya,

    What a marvelous time Dixie, Suzanna, and I had at your home Tues. I feel so blessed to have found you and to be enlightened as to Dixie's thoughts and needs. The visit with my husband was completely unexpected and so precious to me. Listening to the tape I realized I had forgotten to pay for it. So enclosed is my donation to your wonderful work with homeless pets.

    Love,

    Phyllis and Dixie

NOTE FROM RON:

Dear Sonya,

Thank you so very much for your consultation last Wednesday evening regarding Sheba and Molly.

The discussion that I had with you proved further that I do have a positive caring communication between Sheba, Molly, and myself.

Best regards,

Ron T.

LETTER FROM DENISE AFTER CONSULTATION ABOUT HER HORSE:

Dear Sonya,

I have been practicing my skill as a psychic for the last twenty-two years. I have found three missing people, and helped the families bring closure on their losses as well as offer bereavement sessions to clients who have lost loved ones. I am able to contact the deceased and offer peace to those in pain. I offer regular psychic readings to those in need of a job change or hints about a new love interest. That service I accept a fee for. My bereavements I never did until about two years ago. Although I have made an agreement with the universe that I could never accept money for bereavements, I began to ask my clients to donate money to the animal welfare league of their choice in exchange for the reading. Everyone has been extremely receptive to this and I feel as though my energy is being utilized in the best good of all God's creatures. I have a spot on a radio show in Chicago where I offer advice to callers, as well as on a Rockford radio station. I am writing a book and things are beginning to take off for me. (I have a weekly television spot on our CBS affiliate here in Rockford.)

I wanted to tell you a little bit about myself before I told you who I am. I received a reading from you last Wednesday. My name is Denise Guzzardo. Being a psychic, I love to get readings from others. However, I must say I have never enjoyed nor have I been as extremely moved until the reading you gave me the other day. No one has ever been able to touch my heart quite like you did. I have sung your praises to nearly every one of my animal friends about your accuracy and sensitivity toward me and the love I have for my pets. I have recommended your book to many, and don't be surprised if a couple of my DJ friends call you to be on the air. I am able to read other horses but not my own. You verified for me what I thought was my imagination. I shared the story with my sons and they can't wait to hear the tape. You are an angel and may God always bless you and yours.

Sincerely,

Denise Guzzardo

P.S. I would love to meet you. Do you teach clinics or have a web page?

LETTER FROM MARY CLARK ABOUT THE RACEHORSE
RECKLESS AND EASY: AUGUST 1, 1999

Dear Sonya,

Just a little THANK YOU for your help with my quarter horse, Reckless and Easy. After countless trips to the vet, we were about to give up on this three-year-old racehorse. She was terribly headshy, and would flip over backward with no provocation. Then she developed what was thought to be a sinus abscess. But I was not convinced.

After talking to you, you advised that she was in terrible pain on the right side of her face. That it was not related to her teeth or anything you had ever experienced . . . but it was very bad.

So, I convinced my owners to have her entire face X-rayed. The vets at A&M did not feel it was necessary . . . but we insisted it be done. Well, embedded on the RIGHT side of her upper jaw line, between her jawbone and nostril area was a one and one-quarter inch long piece of panic release snap. They guessed it had been there for six months to a year. And they expressed the fact that the pain must have been horrible every time a bridle, halter, or anything was on her face.

Sonya, I can't imagine the cruelty that must have taken place in her lifetime as a young horse. But what is worse, is, had we gotten rid of her and someone else had tried to train her, she could have conceivably killed herself, by flipping. No one would have found that horrible problem.

I can't thank you enough for helping to restore a normal, comfortable life to this horse. It will take some time for her to get over the mental habits she has, but I am happy to say, she is a different horse. She is training very well and is beginning to trust others around her. Thank you again.

I had tried to photograph the awful piece of metal, but it just didn't come out. So I have drawn an outline of it, to give you an idea of what they found.

God Bless you and your family,

Mary Clark

CARD FROM KENAN AND JAN:

Sonya,

Kenan and I enjoyed our "visit" with Morganna and Melissa and the invisible guys Merlin and Smort. We have added Melan, a young black tabby boy to play with Melissa. Morganna has lost her voice—I guess she is feeling powerless and overpowered. You provide such a great service for people and animals.

And Emily! What a woman. Thanks for your communications with her too.

Love,

Jan

EMAIL:
SUBJECT: LOST TAIWAY STORY
DATE: 12/21/00
FROM: RONA AND PETER

Dear Sonya and Denis Fitzpatrick,

The following is the Lost Taiway Story. We hope it will be of use for Sonya's latest book. Please let us know when the new book comes out and if our story makes it on Larry King Live or any other publicity.

Lost Taiway Story:

On the night of 14 August 2000, Rona let our cat Taiway out at around 9.30 P.M. By 3 A.M. we were concerned that Taiway was not waiting by the sliding doors to be let in and started to get worried. It is not like Taiway to wander too far and to be so late. Taiway is the type of cat who runs inside when a car drives by. We looked for Taiway on the streets, in alleys, talked to neighbors, posted the area extensively for weeks, and checked the animal shelter repeatedly. We had been reassured by the city workers that there had not been any dead cats picked up off the streets during the first week of Taiway's disappearance. We received many calls but none of the cats turned out to be Taiway.

It should be noted that Taiway had a collar on with a tag and phone number to call.

In early September, we contacted an animal communica-

tor. She told us that Taiway was alive and that a couple
had her. Furthermore, Taiway roughly told us the path she
took that night and that she had a desire to come home. The
animal communicator also said that the couple adore her,
do not want to give her up, and that Taiway was not far
(within five blocks). We basically believed the information
related to us by this animal communicator as most of the
details she described about our home and Taiway matched
up. Although we did find it odd that Taiway would go with
strangers as she's not very friendly and that this couple
would keep a cat with a tag. We hoped that Taiway would
find a way to escape and come home.

A few weeks passed when we decided to contact another
animal communicator as a last attempt to track down Taiway. We were referred to Sonya Fitzpatrick by an animal
communicator who does not find lost pets.

On October 28, we were completely surprised and sometimes amused by what Taiway related to us through Sonya.
For instance, Taiway told us that she is a beautiful cat.
Sonya mentioned several incidents that occurred in the past
six years that only Taiway would know. By the end of the
session, we learned that contrary to the other animal communicator, Taiway was living on the streets with other stray
cats, and eating food left by animal lovers in the neighborhood. When asked if she had ever been in someone's home,
she said that she would not let just anyone take her. The
problem was basically that she was too nervous to come

home because of a dog and cat that live downstairs from us. The cat had warned her that she was in her territory. We reassured Taiway that because of the colder weather the dog and cat would most likely not be there anymore and that she should come home. Sonya told us she knew her way home and that she would keep telling Taiway to come home.

Four nights after talking to Sonya, Rona got up to comfort our crying daughter at around 1 A.M. She brought her out to the living room from which she saw a shadow of a cat appear at the sliding doors of our balcony. A couple of cats had shown up at our balcony during Taiway's disappearance but Rona knew this was the shadow of her adored cat Taiway. Rona ran to the doors with baby in arms and managed to get the door open in the total darkness only to find that Taiway was no longer there. In fact, she had run down one level of the fire escape. Rona kneeled down on the concrete and put out her hand to Taiway and said "Titi Titi" as we'd nicknamed her. Taiway looked up and meowed her raspy meow a few times. Rona repeated this gesture several more times until Taiway came up the stairs for a pat and followed her into the apartment. She alternated between eating her food hungrily and getting patted. Rona and our daughter were ecstatic. Rona phoned Peter right away as he was out looking for Taiway. He was thrilled at our precious cat's return. The next day Peter called Sonya and Denis Fitzpatrick to tell them the good news and to thank Sonya for her angelic powers.

Our very missed cat Taiway was back in our home almost twelve weeks after her disappearance. Though I wish we had known Sonya the day Taiway first disappeared, Taiway did teach us not to take things for granted.

Rona Harun and Peter Edwards (Taiway's owners)

Index